Quick fixes from brand name mixes

Publications International, Ltd.
Favorite Brand Name Recipes at www.fbnr.com

BISQUICK is a registered trademark of General Mills, Inc.

Ortega is a registered trademarks of Nestlé.

TACO BELL® and HOME ORIGINALS® are trademarks owned and licensed by Taco Bell Corp.

Some of the products listed in this publication may be in limited distribution.

Front cover product photography by Sanders Studios, Inc.

Pictured on the front cover *(clockwise from top left):* Lipton® Onion Burgers *(page 112);* Magic Cookie Bars, Magic Rainbow Cookie Bars *(page 192);* Extra Special Spinach Dip *(page 26);* Fudge Ribbon Cake *(page 174).*

Pictured on the back cover *(top to bottom):* Strawberry Shortcake *(page 200)* and Black Bean and Mango Chicken Salad *(page 66).*

ISBN: 0-7853-8376-X

Library of Congress Control Number: 2002116500

Manufactured in China.

8 7 6 5 4 3 2 1

Microwave Cooking: Microwave ovens vary in wattage. Use the cooking times as guidelines and check for doneness before adding more time.

Preparation/Cooking Times: Preparation times are based on the approximate amount of time required to assemble the recipe before cooking, baking, chilling or serving. These times include preparation steps such as measuring, chopping and mixing. The fact that some preparations and cooking can be done simultaneously is taken into account. Preparation of optional ingredients and serving suggestions is not included.

Contents

Introduction

With today's busy schedules, no one has time to fix meals from scratch. Yet you want to provide nourishing food that tastes good. What's the solution? Fortunately, today's product offerings make fixing meals easier than ever. Prepared, preseasoned, prepackaged and ready-to-use foods let you cut corners without sacrificing taste. Simply mix these time-saving wonders with a few other ingredients, and you can have delicious, wholesome meals in no time.

Inside you'll find a collection of over 180 of the best quick-fix recipes of all time. Now you can enjoy the taste of home-cooked meals—without all the fuss.

Appetizers & Snacks
Whether you're looking for the perfect appetizer to serve at your next party or simply a quick snack to fill a hungry belly, you'll find it in this chapter. Spicy snack mixes, hearty dips, savory skewers and other taste-tempting finger foods—they're all here.

Hot & Hearty Spoonfuls
You'll be amazed to find what the simple addition of a few fresh ingredients and an occasional seasoning packet mix can do for an ordinary can of soup. This chapter's filled with satisfyingly scrumptious, piping-hot soups that taste homemade—but take only a fraction of the time.

Splendor o' Salads
When salads come to mind, you probably think mixed greens with dressing, but salads don't have to be so predictable. Check out this magnificent array which includes everything from Oriental Steak Salad to Sunset Yogurt Salad.

One-Dish Extravaganza

What could be easier than a whole meal served up in a single dish? Choose from home-style casseroles, sizzling stir-fries and fiery skillet meals. You'll have all the necessary components to make up an entire meal in one convenient dish.

Fire Up the Grill!

Get ready to take your grill to new culinary heights! From seafood and burgers to poultry and vegetables, flavorful seasoning mixes and marinades add just the right amount of zest and zing to make these grilled creations some of the best ever.

All-Time Favorites

With the help of a few special mixes, you can serve up the taste of old-fashioned, down-home cooking in no time. Hearty spaghetti and meatballs, creamy turkey tetrazzini, and meaty and saucy lasagna—you'll find all your time-tested favorites in this chapter.

Sides of All Kinds

If you're tired of serving bland, boring vegetables simply because you don't have time to prepare anything more, try some of these creative new ideas. Pick from a medley of no-fuss scrumptious sides sure to complement main dishes of all kinds and add excitement to any meal.

Moist & Luscious Cakes

Take an ordinary cake mix, add a few simple ingredients, and what do you get? The most delectable melt-in-your-mouth taste sensation ever. This chapter features a spectacular array of creative new takes on cakes, cheesecakes, coffeecakes and cupcakes. And best of all? With the help of a mix, they're "a piece of cake" to make!

More Sweets, Please!

A pudding mix to make a pie? A cake mix for cookies? While it sounds outrageous, these fast-fixin' recipes are the simplest way to some of the most decadent desserts. Creamy pies, luscious pudding desserts and rich, fudgy brownies are just a sampling of the tantalizing treats you'll find.

Appetizers & Snacks

Roasted Red Pepper Spread

Makes 2 cups

1 cup roasted red peppers, rinsed and drained
1 package (8 ounces) cream cheese, softened
1 packet (1 ounce) HIDDEN VALLEY® The Original Ranch®
   Salad Dressing & Seasoning Mix
Baguette slices and sliced ripe olives (optional)

Blot dry red peppers. In a food processor fitted with a metal blade,
combine peppers, cream cheese and salad dressing & seasoning mix;
process until smooth. Spread on baguette slices and garnish with
olives, if desired.

Roasted Red Pepper Spread

French-Style Pizza Bites (Pissaladière)

Makes about 24 servings (2 diamonds per serving)

2 tablespoons olive oil
1 medium onion, thinly sliced
1 medium red bell pepper, cut into strips
2 cloves garlic, minced
⅓ cup pitted black olives, each cut into thin wedges
1 can (10 ounces) refrigerated pizza crust dough
¾ cup (3 ounces) finely shredded Swiss or Gruyère cheese

1. Position oven rack to lowest position. Preheat oven to 425°F. Grease large baking sheet.

2. Heat oil until hot in medium skillet over medium heat. Add onion, pepper and garlic. Cook and stir 5 minutes or until vegetables are crisp-tender. Stir in olives; remove from heat.

3. Pat dough into 16×12-inch rectangle on prepared baking sheet.

4. Arrange vegetables over dough; sprinkle with cheese. Bake 10 minutes. Loosen crust from baking sheet; slide crust onto oven rack. Bake 3 to 5 minutes or until golden brown.

5. Slide baking sheet back under crust to remove crust from rack. Transfer to cutting board. Cut dough crosswise into eight 1¾-inch-wide strips. Cut dough diagonally into ten 2-inch-wide strips, making diamond pieces. Serve immediately.

Appetizers & Snacks

French-Style Pizza Bites (Pissaladière)

Classic Chicken Puffs

Makes 6 servings

Prep Time: none
Cook Time: 20 minutes

- 1 box UNCLE BEN'S® Long Grain & Wild Rice Original Recipe
- 2 cups cubed cooked TYSON® Fresh Chicken
- ½ can (10¾ ounces) condensed cream of mushroom soup
- ⅓ cup chopped green onions
- ⅓ cup diced pimientos or diced red bell pepper
- ⅓ cup diced celery
- ⅓ cup chopped fresh parsley
- ⅓ cup chopped slivered almonds
- ¼ cup milk
- 1 box frozen prepared puff pastry shells, thawed

COOK: CLEAN: Wash hands. Prepare rice according to package directions. When rice is done, add remaining ingredients (except pastry shells). Mix well. Reheat 1 minute. Fill pastry shells with rice mixture.

SERVE: Serve with a mixed green salad and balsamic vinaigrette, if desired.

CHILL: Refrigerate leftovers immediately.

10

Helpful Hint

This recipe is a great way to use up leftover chicken.

Classic Chicken Puff

Hot Artichoke Dip
Makes 3 cups dip

Prep Time: 5 minutes
Bake Time: 30 minutes

> 1 envelope LIPTON® RECIPE SECRETS® Onion Soup Mix*
> 1 can (14 ounces) artichoke hearts, drained and chopped
> 1 cup HELLMANN'S® or BEST FOODS® Mayonnaise
> 1 container (8 ounces) sour cream
> 1 cup shredded Swiss or mozzarella cheese (about 4 ounces)

*Also terrific with LIPTON® RECIPE SECRETS® Savory Herb with Garlic, Golden Onion, or Onion-Mushroom Soup Mix.

1. Preheat oven to 350°F. In 1-quart casserole, combine all ingredients.

2. Bake uncovered 30 minutes or until heated through.

3. Serve with your favorite dippers.

Cold Artichoke Dip: Omit Swiss cheese. Stir in, if desired, ¼ cup grated Parmesan cheese. Do not bake.

Helpful Hint

When serving Hot Artichoke Dip for a party, try baking it in two smaller casseroles. When the first casserole is empty, replace it with the second one, fresh from the oven.

Appetizers & Snacks

Hot Artichoke Dip

Spring Vegetable Pie

Makes about 6 servings

Prep Time: 10 minutes
Cook Time: 50 minutes

    4 eggs
  1½ cups milk
    1 cup shredded Swiss cheese (about 4 ounces)
    1 package (10 ounces) frozen chopped spinach, thawed and squeezed dry
    1 package KNORR® Recipe Classics™ Spring Vegetable Soup, Dip and Recipe Mix
    1 (9-inch) frozen deep-dish pie crust

• Preheat oven and cookie sheet to 350°F.

• In large bowl, with wire whisk, beat eggs lightly. Blend in milk, cheese, spinach and recipe mix. Pour into frozen pie crust.

• Bake on cookie sheet 50 minutes or until knife inserted halfway between center and edge comes out clean.

Roasted Eggplant Dip

Makes 2 cups dip

Prep Time: 10 minutes
Cook Time: 50 minutes
Chill Time: 2 hours

    2 medium eggplants, about 1 pound each
    1 package KNORR® Recipe Classics™ Roasted Garlic Herb Soup, Dip and Recipe Mix
  ⅓ to ½ cup olive oil
    2 tablespoons lemon juice
  ¼ cup chopped fresh parsley
    6 (8-inch) whole wheat or white pita breads, cut into wedges

• Preheat oven to 400°F. Cut eggplants lengthwise in half. Arrange eggplants in foil-lined baking pan. Bake 50 minutes or until very tender; cool.

• With spoon, scrape eggplant from skins and place in food processor.* Add recipe mix, oil and lemon juice. Process until smooth; chill 2 hours.

• Stir in parsley just before serving. Serve with pita wedges.

Or, chop on cutting board with knife.

Appetizers & Snacks

Spring Vegetable Pie

Party Stuffed Pinwheels

Makes 32 pinwheels

Prep Time: 10 minutes
Cook Time: 13 minutes

1 envelope LIPTON® RECIPE SECRETS® Ranch Soup Mix*
1 package (8 ounces) cream cheese, softened
1 cup shredded mozzarella cheese (about 4 ounces)
1 tablespoon grated Parmesan cheese
2 tablespoons milk
2 packages (10 ounces each) refrigerated pizza crust

*Also terrific with LIPTON® RECIPE SECRETS® Savory Herb with Garlic or Onion Soup Mix.

1. Preheat oven to 425°F. In medium bowl, combine all ingredients except pizza crust; set aside.

2. Unroll pizza crusts, then evenly top with filling. Roll, starting at longest side, jelly-roll style. Cut into 32 rounds.*

3. On baking sheet sprayed with nonstick cooking spray, arrange rounds cut side down.

4. Bake uncovered 13 minutes or until golden brown.

16

*If rolled pizza crust is too soft to cut, refrigerate or freeze until firm.

Appetizers & Snacks

Party Stuffed Pinwheels

Cheddar Cheese and Rice Roll

Makes 15 servings

Prep Time: 20 minutes
Cook Time: none

2 cups cooked UNCLE BEN'S® ORIGINAL CONVERTED® Brand Rice
3 cups grated low-fat Cheddar cheese
¾ cup fat-free cream cheese, softened
1 can (4½ ounces) green chilies, drained, chopped
⅛ teaspoon hot sauce
1½ cups chopped walnuts

PREP: CLEAN: Wash hands. Combine rice, Cheddar cheese, cream cheese, chilies and hot sauce. Mix by hand or in food processor. Shape mixture into a log. Roll in walnuts. Wrap tightly with plastic wrap and refrigerate 1 hour.

SERVE: Serve with assorted crackers.

CHILL: Refrigerate leftovers immediately.

Ranch-Style Crab Caliente

Makes 8 to 10 servings

1 package (8 ounces) cream cheese, softened
1 cup mayonnaise
1 packet (.4 ounce) HIDDEN VALLEY® The Original Ranch® Buttermilk Recipe Salad Dressing Mix
2 tablespoons lemon juice
1 large tomato, seeded and chopped
½ cup chopped green onions
6 ounces fresh or canned crabmeat
1 tablespoon diced seeded jalapeño pepper
Parsley and paprika

Preheat oven to 350°F. In medium bowl, blend cream cheese, mayonnaise, salad dressing mix and lemon juice until smooth. Stir in tomato, green onions, crabmeat and jalapeño. Spoon mixture into small casserole dish; bake 15 minutes. Remove from oven, garnish with parsley and lightly dust surface with paprika. Serve immediately with fresh bread or crackers.

Appetizers & Snacks

Cheddar Cheese and Rice Roll

7-Layer Sombrero Dip

Makes 8 to 10 servings

    1 can (16 ounces) refried beans
    1 container (8 ounces) sour cream (1 cup)
    1 packet (1 ounce) HIDDEN VALLEY® The Original Ranch® Dips Mix
    1 cup diced tomatoes
    1 can (4 ounces) diced green chiles, rinsed and drained
    1 can (2¼ ounces) sliced ripe olives, rinsed and drained
    ¾ cup (3 ounces) shredded Cheddar cheese
    ¾ cup (3 ounces) shredded Monterey Jack cheese
    Chopped avocado (optional)
    Tortilla chips, for dipping

Spread beans on a 10-inch serving platter. Blend sour cream and dips mix. Spread over beans. Layer tomatoes, chiles, olives, Cheddar cheese, Monterey Jack cheese and avocado, if desired. Serve with tortilla chips.

Stuffed Mushrooms

Makes 12 appetizer servings

    1 package (6 ounces) STOVE TOP® Chicken Flavor Stuffing Mix
    24 large mushrooms (about 1½ pounds)
    ¼ cup (½ stick) butter or margarine
    ¼ cup each finely chopped red and green pepper
    3 tablespoons butter or margarine, melted

Prepare Stuffing Mix Pouch as directed on package, omitting butter. Remove stems from mushrooms; chop stems. Melt ¼ cup butter in skillet. Add mushroom caps; cook and stir until lightly browned. Arrange in shallow baking pan. Cook and stir chopped mushroom stems and peppers in skillet until tender; stir into prepared stuffing. Spoon onto mushroom caps; drizzle with 3 tablespoons butter. Place under preheated broiler for 5 minutes to heat through.

Appetizers & Snacks

Creamy California Pockets

Makes 16 appetizers

Prep Time: 15 minutes
Cook Time: 13 minutes

    1 envelope LIPTON® RECIPE SECRETS® Onion Soup Mix
    1 box (10 ounces) frozen chopped spinach, thawed and squeezed dry
    2 cups shredded mozzarella cheese (about 8 ounces)
    1 cup sour cream
    ½ teaspoon garlic powder
    ¼ teaspoon ground black pepper
    2 packages (8 ounces each) refrigerated crescent rolls

1. Preheat oven to 350°F. In medium bowl, combine soup mix, spinach, mozzarella cheese, sour cream, garlic powder and pepper.

2. Separate dough into rectangles according to package directions. Place 1 heaping tablespoon of mixture near thickest end of rectangles. Roll towards the point. Bring up the two loose ends and secure dough. Arrange on baking sheet.

3. Bake 13 to 15 minutes or until golden brown.

Refreshers

Makes 4 servings

Preparation Time: 5 minutes
Refrigerating Time: 4 hours

    1 cup boiling water
    1 package (4-serving size) JELL-O® Brand Gelatin Dessert, any flavor
    1 cup cold beverage, such as seltzer, club soda, ginger ale, iced tea or
        lemon-lime carbonated beverage

STIR boiling water into gelatin in medium bowl at least 2 minutes until completely dissolved. Stir in cold beverage.

REFRIGERATE 4 hours or until firm. Cut into cubes and garnish as desired.

Sugar Free Low Calorie Refreshers: Prepare recipe as directed above, using any flavor JELL-O® Brand Sugar Free Low Calorie Gelatin Dessert and 1 cup seltzer, club soda, diet ginger ale, diet iced tea or diet lemon-lime carbonated beverage.

Appetizers & Snacks

Hidden Valley® Salsa Ranch Dip

Makes 2½ cups

   1 container (16 ounces) sour cream (2 cups)
   1 packet (1 ounce) HIDDEN VALLEY® The Original Ranch® Dips Mix
   ½ cup thick and chunky salsa
      Chopped tomatoes and diced green chiles (optional)
      Tortilla chips, for dipping

Combine sour cream and dips mix. Stir in salsa. Add tomatoes and chiles, if desired. Chill 1 hour. Serve with tortilla chips.

Ortega® Snack Mix

Makes about 20 servings

   3 cups lightly salted peanuts
   3 cups corn chips
   3 cups spoon-size shredded wheat cereal
   2 cups lightly salted pretzels
   1 package (1.25 ounces) ORTEGA® Taco Seasoning Mix
   ¼ cup (½ stick) butter or margarine, melted

COMBINE peanuts, corn chips, shredded wheat, pretzels, seasoning mix and butter in large bowl; toss well to coat. Store in airtight container or zipper-type plastic bag.

Hidden Valley® Salsa Ranch Dip

Savory Chicken Satay

Makes 12 to 16 appetizers

Prep Time: 15 minutes
Marinate Time: 30 minutes
Cook Time: 8 minutes

> 1 envelope LIPTON® RECIPE SECRETS® Onion Soup Mix
> ¼ cup olive or vegetable oil
> 2 tablespoons firmly packed brown sugar
> 2 tablespoons SKIPPY® Peanut Butter
> 1 pound boneless, skinless chicken breasts, pounded and cut into thin strips
> 12 to 16 wooden skewers, soaked in water

1. In large plastic bag, combine soup mix, oil, brown sugar and peanut butter. Add chicken and toss to coat well. Close bag and marinate in refrigerator 30 minutes.

2. Remove chicken from marinade, discarding marinade. On large skewers, thread chicken, weaving back and forth.

3. Grill or broil chicken until chicken is no longer pink. Serve with your favorite dipping sauces.

24

Helpful Hint

To pound chicken, place the breasts between two pieces of plastic wrap. This will prevent the chicken from tearing. Using the flat bottom (not the edge) of a meat pounder or a rolling pin, pound the chicken with a downward motion until it is evenly flattened.

Savory Chicken Satay

Extra Special Spinach Dip

Makes 3 cups dip

1 envelope LIPTON® RECIPE SECRETS® Vegetable Soup Mix*
1 container (8 ounces) regular or light sour cream
1 cup regular or light mayonnaise
1 package (10 ounces) frozen chopped spinach, thawed and squeezed dry
1 can (8 ounces) water chestnuts, drained and chopped (optional)

*Also terrific with LIPTON® RECIPE SECRETS® Savory Herb with Garlic Soup Mix.

1. In medium bowl, combine all ingredients; chill at least 2 hours.

2. Serve with your favorite dippers.

Hot 'n' Spicy Italian Stix Mix

Makes 7 cups mix

Prep Time: 15 minutes
Cook Time: 30 minutes

6 tablespoons butter or margarine, melted
2 tablespoons *Frank's*® *RedHot*® Cayenne Pepper Sauce
1 tablespoon *French's*® Worcestershire Sauce
2⅔ cups *French's*® French Fried Onions, divided
2 cans (1½ ounces each) *French's*® Potato Sticks
4 cups oven-toasted rice cereal squares
1 package (1.25 ounces) Italian spaghetti sauce mix
¼ cup grated Parmesan cheese

1. Preheat oven to 250°F. Combine butter, ***Frank's RedHot*** Sauce and Worcestershire in glass measuring cup. Place remaining ingredients in shallow roasting pan; mix well. Pour butter mixture over cereal mixture; toss to coat evenly.

2. Bake 30 minutes or until crispy, stirring twice. Cool completely.

26

Appetizers & Snacks

Extra Special Spinach Dip

Bite Size Tacos

Makes 8 appetizer servings

Prep Time: 5 minutes
Cook Time: 15 minutes

> 1 pound ground beef
> 1 package (1.25 ounces) taco seasoning mix
> 2 cups *French's®* French Fried Onions
> ¼ cup chopped fresh cilantro
> 32 bite-size round tortilla chips
> ¾ cup sour cream
> 1 cup shredded Cheddar cheese

1. Cook beef in nonstick skillet over medium-high heat 5 minutes or until browned; drain. Stir in taco seasoning mix, *¾ cup water, 1 cup* French Fried Onions and cilantro. Simmer 5 minutes or until flavors are blended, stirring often.

2. Preheat oven to 350°F. Arrange tortilla chips on foil-lined baking sheet. Top with beef mixture, sour cream, remaining onions and cheese.

3. Bake 5 minutes or until cheese is melted and onions are golden.

Helpful Hint

Serve these mini-tacos with diced fresh tomato, olives, refried beans and lettuce for even more flavor and variety.

Appetizers & Snacks

Bite Size Tacos

Hidden Valley® Bacon-Cheddar Ranch Dip

Makes about 3 cups

1 container (16 ounces) sour cream (2 cups)
1 packet (1 ounce) HIDDEN VALLEY® The Original Ranch® Dips Mix
1 cup (4 ounces) shredded Cheddar cheese
¼ cup crisp-cooked, crumbled bacon*
Potato chips or corn chips, for dipping

Bacon pieces may be used.

Combine sour cream and dips mix. Stir in cheese and bacon. Garnish as desired. Chill at least 1 hour. Serve with chips.

Original Ranch® Meatballs

Makes 2 dozen meatballs

1 pound ground beef
1 packet (1 ounce) HIDDEN VALLEY® The Original Ranch® Salad Dressing
    & Seasoning Mix
2 tablespoons butter or margarine
½ cup beef broth

Combine ground beef and salad dressing & seasoning mix. Shape into meatballs. Melt butter in a skillet; brown meatballs on all sides. Add broth; cover and simmer 10 to 15 minutes or until cooked through. Serve warm with toothpicks.

Appetizers & Snacks

Hidden Valley® Bacon-Cheddar Ranch Dip

Hot French Onion Dip

Makes 2 cups dip

1 envelope LIPTON® RECIPE SECRETS® Onion Soup Mix
1 container (16 ounces) sour cream
2 cups shredded Swiss cheese (about 8 ounces)
¼ cup HELLMAN'S® or BEST FOODS® Mayonnaise

1. Preheat oven to 375°F. In 1-quart casserole, combine soup mix, sour cream, 1¾ cups Swiss cheese and mayonnaise.

2. Bake uncovered 20 minutes or until heated through. Sprinkle with remaining ¼ cup cheese.

3. Serve, if desired, with sliced French bread or your favorite dippers.

Polenta Triangles

Makes about 24 triangles

3 cups cold water
1 cup yellow cornmeal
1 envelope LIPTON® RECIPE SECRETS® Golden Onion or Onion Soup Mix
1 can (4 ounces) mild chopped green chilies, drained
½ cup thawed frozen or drained canned whole kernel corn
⅓ cup finely chopped roasted red peppers
½ cup shredded sharp Cheddar cheese (about 2 ounces)

In 3-quart saucepan, bring water to a boil over high heat. With wire whisk, stir in cornmeal, then golden onion soup mix. Reduce heat to low and simmer uncovered, stirring constantly, 25 minutes or until thickened. Stir in chilies, corn and roasted red peppers.

Spread into lightly greased 9-inch square baking pan; sprinkle with cheese. Let stand 20 minutes or until firm; cut into triangles. Serve at room temperature or heat in oven at 350°F for 5 minutes or until warm.

Appetizers & Snacks

Hot French Onion Dip

Baked Spinach Balls

Makes 12 servings

2 cups sage and onion or herb-seasoned bread stuffing mix
2 tablespoons grated Parmesan cheese
1 small onion, chopped
1 clove garlic, minced
¼ teaspoon dried thyme leaves
¼ teaspoon black pepper
1 package (10 ounces) frozen chopped spinach, thawed and well drained
¼ cup fat-free reduced-sodium chicken broth
2 egg whites, beaten
  Dijon or honey mustard (optional)

1. Combine stuffing mix, cheese, onion, garlic, thyme and pepper in medium bowl; mix well. Combine spinach, broth and egg whites in separate medium bowl; mix well. Stir into bread cube mixture. Cover; refrigerate 1 hour or until mixture is firm.

2. Preheat oven to 350°F. Shape mixture into 24 balls. Place on ungreased baking sheet; bake 15 minutes or until spinach balls are browned. Serve with mustard for dipping, if desired. Garnish, if desired.

Sausage Cheese Puffs

Makes about 60 appetizers

1 pound BOB EVANS® Original Recipe Roll Sausage
2½ cups (10 ounces) shredded sharp Cheddar cheese
2 cups biscuit mix
½ cup water
1 teaspoon baking powder

Preheat oven to 350°F. Combine ingredients in large bowl until blended. Shape into 1-inch balls. Place on lightly greased baking sheets. Bake about 25 minutes or until golden brown. Serve hot. Refrigerate leftovers.

Appetizers & Snacks

Baked Spinach Balls

Lipton® Ranch Dip

Makes 2 cups dip

Prep Time: 5 minutes

> **1 envelope LIPTON® RECIPE SECRETS® Ranch Soup Mix**
> **1 container (16 ounces) sour cream**

1. In medium bowl, combine ingredients; chill, if desired.

2. Serve with your favorite dippers.

Ranch Salsa Dip: Stir in ½ cup of your favorite salsa.

Ranch Artichoke Dip: Stir in 1 jar (14 ounces) marinated artichoke hearts, drained and chopped.

Lipton® Onion Dip

Makes 2 cups dip

Prep Time: 5 minutes

> **1 envelope LIPTON® RECIPE SECRETS® Onion Soup Mix**
> **1 container (16 ounces) sour cream**

1. In medium bowl, combine ingredients; chill, if desired.

2. Serve with your favorite dippers.

Salsa Onion Dip: Stir in ½ cup of your favorite salsa.

Appetizers & Snacks

Top to bottom: Lipton® Onion Dip, Lipton® Ranch Dip

Herbed Blue Cheese Spread with Garlic Toasts

Makes 16 servings

1⅓ cups 1% low-fat cottage cheese
1¼ cups (5 ounces) crumbled blue, feta or goat cheese
  1 large clove garlic
  2 teaspoons lemon juice
  2 green onions with tops, sliced (about ¼ cup)
  ¼ cup chopped fresh basil or oregano *or* 1 teaspoon dried basil or oregano leaves
  2 tablespoons toasted slivered almonds*
    Garlic Toasts (recipe follows)

To toast almonds, place almonds in shallow baking pan. Bake in preheated 350°F about 10 minutes or until lightly toasted, stirring occasionally. (Watch almonds carefully—they burn easily.)

1. Combine cottage cheese, blue cheese, garlic and lemon juice in food processor; process until smooth. Add green onions, basil and almonds; pulse until well blended but still chunky.

2. Spoon cheese spread into small serving bowl; cover. Refrigerate until ready to serve.

3. When ready to serve, prepare Garlic Toasts. Spread 1 tablespoon cheese spread onto each toast slice. Garnish, if desired.

Garlic Toasts

Makes 32 pieces

32 French bread slices, ½ inch thick
    Nonstick cooking spray
  ¼ teaspoon garlic powder
  ⅛ teaspoon salt

Place bread slices on nonstick baking sheet. Lightly coat both sides of bread slices with cooking spray. Combine garlic powder and salt in small bowl; sprinkle evenly onto bread slices. Broil 6 to 8 inches from heat 30 to 45 seconds on each side or until bread slices are lightly toasted on both sides.

Appetizers & Snacks

Herbed Blue Cheese Spread with Garlic Toasts

Hot & Hearty Spoonfuls

Ranch Clam Chowder
Makes 6 servings

¼ **cup chopped onion**
3 **tablespoons butter or margarine**
½ **pound fresh mushrooms, sliced**
2 **tablespoons Worcestershire sauce**
1½ **cups half-and-half**
1 **can (10¾ ounces) cream of potato soup**
¼ **cup dry white wine**
1 **packet (1 ounce) HIDDEN VALLEY® The Original Ranch® Salad Dressing & Seasoning Mix**
1 **can (10 ounces) whole baby clams, undrained**
Chopped parsley

In 3-quart saucepan, cook onion in butter over medium heat until onion is soft but not browned. Add mushrooms and Worcestershire sauce. Cook until mushrooms are soft and pan juices have almost evaporated. In medium bowl, whisk together half-and-half, potato soup, wine and salad dressing & seasoning mix until smooth. Drain clam liquid into dressing mixture; stir into mushrooms in pan. Cook, uncovered, until soup is heated through but not boiling. Add clams to soup; cook until heated through. Garnish each serving with parsley.

Ranch Clam Chowder

Hearty Minestrone Soup

Makes 6 servings

Prep Time: 10 minutes
Cook Time: 5 minutes

> 2 cans (10¾ ounces each) condensed Italian tomato soup
> 3 cups water
> 3 cups cooked vegetables, such as zucchini, peas, corn or beans
> 2 cups cooked ditalini pasta
> 1⅓ cups *French's®* French Fried Onions

Combine soup and water in large saucepan. Add vegetables and pasta. Bring to a boil. Reduce heat. Cook until heated through, stirring often.

Place French Fried Onions in microwavable dish. Microwave on HIGH 1 minute or until onions are golden.

Ladle soup into individual bowls. Sprinkle with French Fried Onions.

Indian Summer Turkey Soup

Makes 6 (1-cup) servings

> 4 cups water
> 1 envelope LIPTON® Recipe Secrets Noodle Soup Mix with Real Chicken Broth
> ½ pound cooked smoked or regular turkey breast, diced
> 1 small tomato, diced
> ½ cup 1-inch diagonally-cut asparagus
> ½ cup whole kernel corn
> ¼ teaspoon fennel seeds, crushed (optional)

In large saucepan, bring water to a boil. Stir in remaining ingredients. Bring to a boil, then simmer uncovered, stirring occasionally, 5 minutes or until asparagus is tender.

Microwave Directions: In 2-quart microwave-safe casserole, combine water with fennel, if desired. Microwave covered at HIGH (Full Power) 10 minutes or until boiling. Stir in remaining ingredients. Microwave, covered, 7 minutes or until asparagus is tender, stirring once. Let stand, covered, 2 minutes.

Hot & Hearty Spoonfuls

Hearty Minestrone Soup

Mushroom-Beef Stew

Makes 4 servings

1 pound beef stew meat
1 can (10¾ ounces) cream of mushroom soup, undiluted
1 envelope (1 ounce) dry onion soup mix
2 cans (4 ounces each) sliced mushrooms, drained

Slow Cooker Directions

Combine all ingredients in slow cooker. Cover and cook on LOW 8 to 10 hours. Serve over hot cooked noodles and garnish as desired.

Chunky Chicken Noodle Soup with Vegetables

Makes about 4 (1¾-cup) main-dish or 7 (1-cup) appetizer servings

2 envelopes LIPTON® RECIPE SECRETS® Noodle Soup Mix with Real Chicken Broth
6 cups water
½ small head escarole, torn into pieces (about 2 cups)*
1 large stalk celery, sliced
1 small carrot, sliced
¼ cup frozen peas (optional)
1 small clove garlic, finely chopped
½ teaspoon dried thyme leaves, crushed
2 whole cloves
1 bay leaf
2 cups cut-up cooked chicken
1 tablespoon finely chopped parsley

Or substitute 2 cups shredded cabbage.

In large saucepan or stockpot, combine noodle soup mix, water, escarole, celery, carrot, peas, garlic, thyme, cloves and bay leaf. Bring to a boil, then simmer uncovered, stirring occasionally, 15 minutes or until vegetables are tender. Stir in chicken and parsley; heat through. Remove bay leaf.

Microwave Directions: In 3-quart microwave-safe casserole, combine as directed above. Microwave uncovered at HIGH (Full Power), stirring occasionally, 20 minutes or until vegetables are tender. Stir in chicken and parsley; microwave, uncovered, 1 minute or until heated through. Remove bay leaf. Let stand, covered, 5 minutes.

Hot & Hearty Spoonfuls

Mushroom-Beef Stew

Veggie Soup

Makes 4 servings

Prep Time: 2 minutes
Cook Time: 10 to 12 minutes

> 1 bag (16 ounces) BIRDS EYE® frozen Mixed Vegetables
> 1 can (11 ounces) tomato rice soup
> 1 can (10 ounces) French onion soup
> 1 soup can of water

- In large saucepan, cook vegetables according to package directions; drain.

- Add both cans of soup and water; cook over medium-high heat until heated through.

Serving Suggestion: Sprinkle individual servings with ¼ cup shredded Cheddar cheese.

Chicken Soup Parmigiana

Makes about 5 cups

> 3 cups water
> ½ pound boneless chicken breasts, cut into ½-inch pieces
> 1 cup chopped fresh tomatoes *or* 1 can (8 ounces) whole peeled tomatoes, undrained and chopped
> 1 cup sliced zucchini or yellow squash
> 1 envelope LIPTON® Soup Secrets Noodle Soup Mix with Real Chicken Broth
> ½ teaspoon dried oregano leaves (optional)
> ½ teaspoon LAWRY'S® Garlic Powder with Parsley
> ½ teaspoon dried basil leaves* (optional)
> ⅓ cup shredded mozzarella cheese (about 1 ounce)
> Grated Parmesan cheese (optional)

*Or, use 2 teaspoons chopped fresh basil leaves.

In medium saucepan, combine all ingredients except cheese. Bring to a boil; simmer, stirring occasionally, 5 minutes or until chicken is no longer pink. Spoon into bowls; sprinkle, if desired, with mozzarella cheese and grated Parmesan cheese.

Microwave Directions: In 2-quart microwave-safe casserole, combine all ingredients except zucchini and cheese; stir thoroughly. Microwave at HIGH 5 minutes, stirring once. Stir in zucchini. Microwave at HIGH uncovered 11 minutes or until chicken is done; stir. Serve as above.

Hot & Hearty Spoonfuls

Veggie Soup

Avocado Ranch Soup

Makes 6 servings

>**1 cup milk**
>**¾ cup plain lowfat yogurt**
>**¼ cup mayonnaise**
>**1 can (14½ ounces) chicken broth**
>**1 packet (1 ounce) HIDDEN VALLEY® The Original Ranch® Salad Dressing & Seasoning Mix**
>**1 large ripe avocado, cut into chunks**
>**1 medium tomato, diced**
>**½ unpared cucumber, seeded and diced**
>**¼ cup finely diced purple onion**
>**Avocado slices**

In blender, combine milk, yogurt, mayonnaise, chicken broth, salad dressing & seasoning mix and avocado chunks. Purée until smooth. Pour mixture into large bowl. Stir in tomato, cucumber and onion. Cover and refrigerate at least 4 hours. Garnish each bowl with avocado slices before serving.

7-Spice Chili with Corn Bread Topping

Makes 6 servings

>**1 pound ground turkey *or* lean beef**
>**1 jar (16 ounces) Original *or* Spicy TABASCO® brand 7-Spice Chili Recipe**
>**1 can (16 ounces) kidney beans, rinsed and drained**
>**¾ cup water**
>**1 package (12 ounces) corn muffin mix**
>**1 can (7 ounces) whole kernel corn with sweet green and red peppers, drained**
>**1 cup (4 ounces) shredded Cheddar cheese**

In large skillet, brown turkey; drain. Stir in TABASCO® 7-Spice Chili Recipe, beans and water. Bring to a boil; reduce heat. Simmer 10 minutes.

Divide evenly among 6 (12-ounce) individual ramekins.

Meanwhile, prepare corn muffin mix according to package directions. Stir in corn and cheese until well blended.

Pour about ½ cup muffin mixture over top of each ramekin. Bake at 400°F 15 minutes or until corn bread topping is golden brown.

Hot & Hearty Spoonfuls

Avocado Ranch Soup

Country Chicken Stew with Dumplings

Makes about 6 servings

 1 tablespoon BERTOLLI® Olive Oil
 1 chicken (3 to 3½ pounds), cut into serving pieces (with or without skin)
 4 large carrots, cut into 2-inch pieces
 3 ribs celery, cut into 1-inch pieces
 1 large onion, cut into 1-inch wedges
 1 envelope LIPTON® RECIPE SECRETS® Savory Herb with Garlic Soup Mix*
1½ cups water
 ½ cup apple juice
    Parsley Dumplings, optional (recipe follows)

*Also terrific with LIPTON® RECIPE SECRETS® Golden Onion Soup Mix.

In 6-quart Dutch oven or heavy saucepot, heat oil over medium-high heat and brown ½ of the chicken; remove and set aside. Repeat with remaining chicken. Return chicken to Dutch oven. Stir in carrots, celery, onion and savory herb with garlic soup mix blended with water and apple juice. Bring to a boil over high heat. Reduce heat to low and simmer covered 25 minutes or until chicken is done and vegetables are tender.

Meanwhile, prepare Parsley Dumplings. Drop 12 rounded tablespoonfuls of batter into simmering broth around chicken. Continue simmering covered 10 minutes or until toothpick inserted in center of dumpling comes out clean. Season stew, if desired, with salt and pepper.

Parsley Dumplings: In medium bowl, combine 1⅓ cups all-purpose flour, 2 teaspoons baking powder, 1 tablespoon chopped fresh parsley and ½ teaspoon salt; set aside. In measuring cup, blend ⅔ cup milk, 2 tablespoons melted butter or margarine and 1 egg. Stir milk mixture into flour mixture just until blended.

Variation: Add 1 pound quartered red potatoes to stew with carrots; eliminate dumplings.

Country Chicken Stew with Dumplings

Creamy Leek Chowder

Makes 4 servings

Prep Time: 10 minutes
Cook Time: 10 minutes

    1 package (1.8 ounces) leek soup mix
  2¼ cups water
  1½ cups milk
    1 can (14.5 ounces) whole new potatoes, drained and cut into small cubes
  1⅓ cups *French's*® French Fried Onions, divided
    2 teaspoons chopped fresh thyme *or* ½ teaspoon dried thyme leaves
    ¼ teaspoon ground black pepper
      Sour cream
      Chopped parsley

Combine soup mix, water and milk in large saucepan; whisk until well blended. Stir in potatoes, *1 cup* French Fried Onions, thyme and pepper. Bring to a boil over medium-high heat. Reduce heat to low. Simmer, uncovered, 10 minutes, stirring occasionally.

Ladle into individual bowls. Top with sour cream, parsley and remaining ⅓ *cup* onions.

Tip: To crisp and brown French Fried Onions, place on paper towels and microwave on HIGH 1 minute.

Mexicali Vegetable Soup

Makes 6 to 8 servings

    ½ pound ground beef
    ½ cup chopped onion
  3½ cups (two 15-ounce cans) beef broth
  1¾ cups (14½-ounce can) small white beans, drained
    1 cup (1 large) sliced zucchini
    1 cup frozen sliced carrots
    1 package (1¼ ounces) ORTEGA® Taco Seasoning Mix

COOK beef and onion in large saucepan until beef is browned; drain. Add broth, beans, zucchini, carrots and seasoning mix. Bring to a boil. Reduce heat to low; cook, covered, for 15 to 20 minutes.

Hearty Lentil Stew

Makes about 4 servings

- 2 tablespoons BERTOLLI® Olive Oil
- 3 medium carrots, sliced
- 3 ribs celery, sliced
- 1 cup lentils
- 3 cups water, divided
- 1 envelope LIPTON® RECIPE SECRETS® Savory Herb with Garlic Soup Mix*
- 1 tablespoon cider vinegar or red wine vinegar
- Hot cooked brown rice, couscous or pasta

Also terrific with LIPTON® RECIPE SECRETS® Onion-Mushroom or Onion Soup Mix.

In 3-quart saucepan, heat oil over medium heat and cook carrots and celery, stirring occasionally, 3 minutes. Add lentils and cook 1 minute. Stir in 2 cups water. Bring to a boil over high heat. Reduce heat to low and simmer covered, stirring occasionally, 25 minutes. Stir in soup mix blended with remaining 1 cup water. Simmer covered additional 10 minutes or until lentils are tender. Stir in vinegar. Serve over hot rice.

Burgundy Beef Stew

Makes 4 servings

- ¾ pound beef sirloin steak, cut into 1-inch cubes
- 1 cup diagonally sliced carrots
- 1 teaspoon minced garlic
- ¼ cup Burgundy or other dry red wine
- 2⅓ cups canned beef broth
- 1 can (14½ ounces) diced tomatoes, undrained
- 1 box UNCLE BEN'S® COUNTRY INN® Rice Pilaf
- 1 jar (15 ounces) whole pearl onions, drained

1. Generously spray large saucepan or Dutch oven with nonstick cooking spray. Heat over high heat until hot. Add beef; cook 2 to 3 minutes or until no longer pink. Stir in carrots, garlic and wine; cook 2 minutes.

2. Add broth, tomatoes, rice and contents of seasoning packet. Bring to a boil. Cover; reduce heat and simmer 10 minutes, stirring occasionally. Add onions; cook 10 minutes more or until rice is tender. Remove from heat and let stand, covered, 5 minutes.

Variation: One 15-ounce can of drained sweet peas and pearl onions can be substituted for the pearl onions.

Bouillabaisse

Makes 6 servings

Prep Time: 15 minutes
Cook Time: 10 minutes

> **2 cups water**
> **1 package KNORR® Recipe Classics™ Vegetable or Spring Vegetable Soup, Dip and Recipe Mix**
> **1 bottle or can (8 to 10 ounces) clam juice**
> **2 teaspoons tomato paste**
> **½ teaspoon paprika**
> **¼ teaspoon saffron threads (optional)**
> **12 mussels or clams, well scrubbed**
> **1½ pounds mixed seafood (cubed cod, snapper, scallops or shrimp)**

• In 3-quart saucepan, bring water, recipe mix, clam juice, tomato paste, paprika and saffron to a boil over medium-high heat, stirring occasionally.

• Add mussels and seafood. Bring to a boil over high heat.

• Reduce heat to low and simmer 5 minutes or until shells open and seafood is cooked through and flakes easily when tested with a fork. Discard any unopened shells.

Creamy Turkey Soup

Makes 4 servings

> **2 tablespoons butter**
> **½ cup chopped onion**
> **1 cup sliced fresh mushrooms**
> **2 packages (.88 ounce each) LAWRY'S® Gravy Mix for Chicken**
> **1 quart milk**
> **1 cup cooked, cubed turkey**
> **⅛ teaspoon white pepper**

In medium saucepan, heat butter. Add onion and mushrooms and cook over medium-high heat until tender. Add Gravy Mix for Chicken and milk, stirring constantly until blended. Add turkey and pepper. Bring to a boil over medium-high heat; reduce heat to low and simmer, uncovered, 3 to 5 minutes.

Serving Suggestion: Sprinkle each serving with paprika for color.

Hot & Hearty Spoonfuls

Bouillabaisse

Fast 'n Easy Chili

Makes 6 servings

   1½ **pounds ground beef**
    1 **envelope LIPTON® RECIPE SECRETS® Onion Soup Mix***
    1 **can (15 to 19 ounces) red kidney or black beans, drained**
   1½ **cups water**
    1 **can (8 ounces) tomato sauce**
    4 **teaspoons chili powder**

Also terrific with LIPTON® RECIPE SECRETS® Beefy Mushroom, Onion-Mushroom or Beefy Onion Soup Mix.

1. In 12-inch skillet, brown ground beef over medium-high heat; drain.

2. Stir in remaining ingredients. Bring to a boil over high heat. Reduce heat to low and simmer covered, stirring occasionally, 20 minutes. Top hot chili with shredded Cheddar cheese, and serve over hot cooked rice, if desired.

First Alarm Chili: Add 5 teaspoons chili powder.

Second Alarm Chili: Add 2 tablespoons chili powder.

Third Alarm Chili: Add chili powder at your own risk.

Wisconsin Cheese 'n' Beer Soup

Makes about 4 (1-cup) servings

    2 **tablespoons butter or margarine**
    2 **tablespoons all-purpose flour**
    1 **envelope LIPTON® RECIPE SECRETS® Golden Onion Soup Mix**
    3 **cups milk**
    1 **teaspoon Worcestershire sauce**
    1 **cup shredded Cheddar cheese (about 4 ounces)**
   ½ **cup beer**
    1 **teaspoon prepared mustard**

In medium saucepan, melt butter and cook flour over medium heat, stirring constantly, 3 minutes or until bubbling. Stir in golden onion soup mix thoroughly blended with milk and Worcestershire sauce. Bring just to the boiling point, then simmer, stirring occasionally, 10 minutes. Stir in remaining ingredients and simmer, stirring constantly, 5 minutes or until cheese is melted. Garnish, if desired, with additional cheese, chopped red pepper and parsley.

Fast 'n Easy Chili

Hearty Mushroom Barley Soup

Makes 4 (1½-cup) servings

    Nonstick cooking spray
1 teaspoon extra-virgin olive oil
2 cups chopped yellow onions
1 cup thinly sliced carrots
2 cans (about 14 ounces each) fat-free reduced-sodium chicken broth
1 can (10¾ ounces) 98% fat-free cream of mushroom soup, undiluted
12 ounces sliced mushrooms
½ cup quick-cooking barley, uncooked
1 teaspoon reduced-sodium Worcestershire sauce
½ teaspoon dried thyme leaves
¼ cup finely chopped green onions
¼ teaspoon salt
¼ teaspoon black pepper

Heat Dutch oven or large saucepan over medium-high heat until hot. Coat with cooking spray. Add oil and tilt pan to coat bottom of pan. Add yellow onions; cook 8 minutes or until just beginning to turn golden. Add carrots and cook 2 minutes.

Add chicken broth, cream of mushroom soup, mushrooms, barley, Worcestershire sauce and thyme; bring to a boil over high heat. Reduce heat to medium-low; cover and simmer 15 minutes, stirring occasionally. Stir in green onions, salt and pepper. Garnish as desired.

Hearty One-Pot Chicken Stew

Makes 4 servings

    12 boneless, skinless chicken tenderloins, cut into 1-inch pieces
1 box UNCLE BEN'S® CHEF'S RECIPE™ Traditional Red Beans & Rice
2¼ cups water
1 can (14½ ounces) diced tomatoes, undrained
3 red potatoes, unpeeled, cut into 1-inch pieces
2 carrots, sliced ½ inch thick
1 onion, cut into 1-inch pieces

In large saucepan, combine chicken, beans & rice, contents of seasoning packet, water, tomatoes, potatoes, carrots and onion. Bring to a boil. Cover; reduce heat and simmer 20 minutes or until vegetables are tender.

Hearty Mushroom Barley Soup

Easy Ham & Veg•All® Chowder

Makes 4 to 6 servings

Prep Time: 7 minutes

> **2 cans (15 ounces each) VEG•ALL® Original Mixed Vegetables, with liquid**
> **1 can (10¾ ounces) cream of potato soup**
> **1 cup cooked ham, cubed**
> **½ teaspoon dried basil**
> **¼ teaspoon black pepper**

In medium saucepan, combine Veg•All, soup, ham, basil, and black pepper. Heat until hot; serve.

Meatball & Pasta Soup

Makes 8 servings

Prep Time: 10 minutes
Cook Time: 15 minutes

> **2 cans (14½ ounces each) chicken broth**
> **4 cups water**
> **1 can (15 ounces) crushed tomatoes**
> **1 package (15 ounces) frozen precooked Italian style meatballs, not in sauce**
> **1 envelope LIPTON® RECIPE SECRETS® Onion Soup Mix**
> **½ teaspoon garlic powder**
> **1 cup uncooked mini pasta (such as conchigliette or ditalini)**
> **4 cups fresh baby spinach leaves**

1. In 6-quart saucepot, bring broth, water, crushed tomatoes, meatballs, soup mix and garlic powder to a boil over medium-high heat.

2. Add pasta and cook 5 minutes or until pasta is almost tender. Stir in spinach. Reduce heat to medium and simmer uncovered 2 minutes or until spinach is wilted and pasta is tender. Serve, if desired, with Parmesan cheese.

Easy Ham & Veg•All® Chowder

Chicken Gumbo

Makes 4 to 6 servings

Prep Time: 5 minutes
Cook Time: 20 minutes

>   3 tablespoons vegetable oil
>   1 pound boneless skinless chicken breasts, cut into 1-inch pieces
>   ½ pound smoked sausage,* cut into ¾-inch slices
>   1 bag (16 ounces) BIRDS EYE® frozen Farm Fresh Mixtures Broccoli, Corn and Red Peppers
>   1 can (14½ ounces) stewed tomatoes
>   1½ cups water

*For a spicy gumbo, use andouille sausage. Any type of kielbasa or turkey kielbasa can also be used.

• Heat oil in large saucepan over high heat. Add chicken and sausage; cook until browned, about 8 minutes.

• Add vegetables, tomatoes and water; bring to boil. Reduce heat to medium; cover and cook 5 to 6 minutes.

Hearty White Bean Soup

Makes about 6 cups soup

>   1 tablespoon BERTOLLI® Olive Oil
>   1 medium onion, chopped
>   2 medium carrots, sliced
>   2 ribs celery, sliced
>   1 clove garlic
>   2 cans (19 ounces each) cannelini or white kidney beans, rinsed and drained
>   1 envelope LIPTON® RECIPE SECRETS® Savory Herb with Garlic Soup Mix
>   2 cups water
>   3 cups coarsely chopped escarole or spinach
>   1 medium tomato, diced
>   ¼ cup crumbled feta cheese (optional)

In 3-quart saucepan, heat oil over medium heat and cook onion, carrots, celery and garlic, stirring occasionally, 5 minutes or until tender. Stir in beans and soup mix blended with water. Bring to a boil over high heat. Reduce heat to low and simmer uncovered 15 minutes or until vegetables are tender. Stir in escarole and tomato and cook 2 minutes or until heated through. Top with cheese.

Chicken Gumbo

Splender o' Salads

Veg•All® Vinaigrette Salad
Makes 4 servings

> 1 can (15 ounces) VEG•ALL® Original Mixed Vegetables, drained
> 1 can (15 ounces) black beans, drained and rinsed
> 1½ cups cherry tomatoes, halved
> 4 green onions, minced
> ½ cup minced fresh parsley
> 1 bottle (8 ounces) Italian salad dressing
> Lettuce

In large mixing bowl, combine Veg•All, beans, tomatoes, green onions and parsley. Pour dressing over vegetables; toss to blend. Cover; refrigerate for at least 2 hours or until chilled. Serve on bed of lettuce.

Veg•All® Vinaigrette Salad

Black Bean and Mango Chicken Salad

Makes 4 servings

Prep: 10 minutes plus refrigerating

> 1 can (16 ounces) black beans, drained, rinsed
> 1 package (10 ounces) frozen corn, thawed
> 1 cup chopped ripe mango
> ½ pound boneless skinless chicken breasts, grilled, cut up
> ½ cup chopped red pepper
> ⅓ cup chopped fresh cilantro
> ⅓ cup chopped red onion
> ¼ cup lime juice
> 1 envelope GOOD SEASONS® Italian Salad Dressing Mix

TOSS all ingredients in large bowl. Refrigerate.

SERVE with baked tortilla chips, if desired.

Helpful Hint

To prepare a mango for chopping, hold it stem-end-up on a cutting board. Use a utility knife to make a vertical cut on the flat side of the mango from the top to the bottom about ½ inch to the right of the stem and seed. Repeat on the opposite flat side of the mango. One pound of mangoes is equal to about 2½ cups peeled and diced fruit.

Splender o' Salads

Black Bean and Mango Chicken Salad

Thai Beef Salad

Makes 4 servings

- ¾ **cup mayonnaise**
- ¾ **cup unsweetened coconut milk**
- 1 **packet (1 ounce) HIDDEN VALLEY® The Original Ranch® Salad Dressing & Seasoning Mix**
- 2 **tablespoons lime juice**
- 1 **pound thinly sliced roast beef**
- 1 **English cucumber, thinly sliced**
- 1 **cup sliced bamboo shoots**
- ¼ **cup cilantro leaves**
- ¼ **cup coarsely chopped peanuts**

Combine mayonnaise, coconut milk, salad dressing & seasoning mix and lime juice in a small bowl; chill 30 minutes. Arrange beef, cucumber, bamboo shoots, if desired, and cilantro on a large platter. Pour dressing in a thin stream over salad. Sprinkle with peanuts.

Veg•All® Caesar Pasta Salad

Makes 4 servings

- 2 **cups cooked rotini pasta**
- 1 **can (15 ounces) VEG•ALL® Original Mixed Vegetables, drained**
- 1 **can (15 ounces) kidney beans, rinsed and drained**
- 1 **cup julienne Swiss cheese strips**
- ¼ **cup prepared Caesar-style salad dressing**
- 1 **teaspoon Italian seasoning**

In large bowl, combine all ingredients and toss lightly. For more robust flavor, refrigerate for 1 to 2 hours before serving.

Thai Beef Salad

Antipasto Salad

Makes 10 to 12 servings

Prep Time: 15 minutes plus refrigerating

1 cup MIRACLE WHIP® Salad Dressing
½ cup milk
2 packages GOOD SEASONS® Italian Salad Dressing Mix
1 package (16 ounces) uncooked mostaccioli, cooked, drained
1 package (8 ounces) OSCAR MAYER® Cotto Salami Slices, cut into strips
1 package (8 ounces) KRAFT® Low-Moisture Part-Skim Mozzarella Cheese, cubed
¾ cup *each* thin red bell pepper strips and thin zucchini strips
½ cup pitted ripe olives, drained, halved

• **MIX** salad dressing, milk, and salad dressing mix in large bowl.

• **ADD** pasta; mix lightly.

• **ARRANGE** remaining ingredients over pasta mixture; cover. Refrigerate several hours or overnight until chilled.

Helpful Hint

To slice a bell pepper, stand it on its end on a cutting board. Cut off 3 to 4 lengthwise slices from the sides with a utility knife, cutting close to, but not through, the stem. Discard the stem and seeds. Scrape out any remaining seeds and rinse the inside of the pepper under cold running water. Slice each piece lengthwise into long strips.

Splender o' Salads

Antipasto Salad

Sunset Yogurt Salad

Makes 5 cups (10 servings)

>   2 packages (4-serving size each) *or* 1 package (8-serving size) JELL-O®
>   Brand Orange or Lemon Flavor Sugar Free Gelatin
>   2 cups boiling water
>   1 container (8 ounces) plain low-fat yogurt
>   ¼ cup cold water
>   1 can (8 ounces) crushed pineapple in unsweetened juice, undrained
>   1 cup shredded carrots

Completely dissolve gelatin in boiling water. Measure 1 cup gelatin into medium mixing bowl; chill until slightly thickened. Stir in yogurt. Pour into medium serving bowl. Chill until set but not firm.

Add cold water to remaining gelatin. Stir in pineapple with juice and carrots. Chill until slightly thickened. Spoon over gelatin-yogurt mixture in bowl. Chill until firm, about 4 hours. Garnish with carrot curl, celery leaf and pineapple slice, if desired.

Warm Chicken Taco Salad

Makes 4 servings

Prep Time: 15 minutes
Cook Time: 10 minutes

>   ½ cup MIRACLE WHIP® or MIRACLE WHIP LIGHT® Dressing, divided
>   4 boneless skinless chicken breast halves (about 1¼ pounds), cut into thin
>   strips
>   1 cup chopped tomato
>   1 package TACO BELL® HOME ORIGINALS®* Taco Seasoning Mix
>   4 cups tortilla chips
>   4 cups shredded lettuce
>   KRAFT® Shredded Sharp Cheddar Cheese
>   Sliced pitted ripe olives
>   Sliced green onion

*TACO BELL and HOME ORIGINALS are registered trademarks owned and licensed by Taco Bell Corp.

• **HEAT** 2 tablespoons of the dressing in large skillet on medium-high heat. Add chicken; cook and stir 5 minutes. Reduce heat to medium; stir in remaining dressing, tomato and seasoning mix.

• **COOK** and stir 5 minutes or until thoroughly heated and chicken is cooked through.

• **LAYER** chips, lettuce and chicken mixture on large platter. Top with cheese, olives and onion.

Sunset Yogurt Salad

Mediterranean Orzo Salad

Makes 4 to 6 servings

SALAD
- 1 cup orzo pasta
- 1 cup diced red bell pepper
- ½ cup crumbled feta cheese
- 1 can (2¼ ounces) sliced ripe olives, rinsed and drained
- ¼ cup chopped fresh basil *or* ½ teaspoon dried basil
    - Fresh basil leaves or parsley sprigs, for garnish (optional)

DRESSING
- 1 packet (1 ounce) HIDDEN VALLEY® The Original Ranch® Salad Dressing & Seasoning Mix
- 3 tablespoons olive oil
- 3 tablespoons red wine vinegar
- 1 teaspoon sugar

Cook orzo according to package directions, omitting salt. Rinse with cold water and drain well. Mix orzo, bell pepper, cheese, olives and chopped fresh basil in a large bowl. (If using dried basil, add to dressing.) Whisk together salad dressing & seasoning mix, oil, vinegar and sugar. Stir dressing into orzo mixture. Cover and refrigerate at least 2 hours. Garnish with basil leaves before serving, if desired.

74

Helpful Hint

The word "orzo" actually means "barley," even though the shape of this pasta looks more like rice. You can find it in the pasta sections of large supermarkets.

Mediterranean Orzo Salad

Oriental Steak Salad

Makes 4 servings

Prep Time: 10 minutes
Cook Time: 12 to 15 minutes

> 1 package (3 ounces) Oriental flavor instant ramen noodles, uncooked
> 4 cups water
> 1 bag (16 ounces) BIRDS EYE® frozen Farm Fresh Mixtures Cauliflower, Carrots & Snow Pea Pods
> 2 tablespoons vegetable oil
> 1 pound boneless beef top loin steak, cut into thin strips
> $\frac{1}{3}$ cup Oriental sesame salad dressing
> $\frac{1}{4}$ cup chow mein noodles
> Lettuce leaves

• Reserve seasoning packet from noodles.

• In large saucepan, bring water to boil. Add ramen noodles and vegetables; return to boil and cook 5 minutes, stirring occasionally. Drain.

• Heat oil in large nonstick skillet over medium-high heat. Add beef; cook and stir about 8 minutes or until browned.

• Stir in reserved seasoning packet until beef is well coated.

• In large bowl, toss together beef, ramen noodles, vegetables and salad dressing. Sprinkle with chow mein noodles. Serve over lettuce.

Serving Suggestion: This salad also can be served chilled. Moisten with additional salad dressing, if necessary. Sprinkle with chow mein noodles and spoon over lettuce just before serving.

Oriental Steak Salad

Vegetable Potato Salad

Makes 6 servings

Prep Time: 20 minutes
Chill Time: 2 hours

> 1 envelope LIPTON® RECIPE SECRETS® Vegetable Soup Mix
> 1 cup HELLMANN'S® or BEST FOODS® Mayonnaise
> 2 teaspoons white vinegar
> 2 pounds red or all-purpose potatoes, cooked and cut into chunks
> ¼ cup red onion, finely chopped (optional)

1. In large bowl, combine soup mix, mayonnaise and vinegar.

2. Add potatoes and onion; toss well. Chill 2 hours.

Fiesta Salad

Makes 4 to 6 servings

> 4 cups shredded lettuce
> 1½ cups cubed pared jicama
> 1 cup tomato wedges
> 1 can (4 ounces) diced green chile peppers
> ⅓ cup thinly sliced green onions with tops
> 1½ cups (6 ounces) shredded Cheddar cheese
> 1 packet (1 ounce) HIDDEN VALLEY® The Original Ranch® Salad Dressing
>   & Seasoning Mix
> 2 cups (1 pint) sour cream
> 1 tablespoon lime juice
> 1 teaspoon chili powder
> 1 tablespoon taco sauce
> 1 ripe avocado, sliced
> 2 cups coarsely crushed tortilla chips

Line salad bowl with shredded lettuce. Fill center with jicama, tomatoes, chile peppers, green onions and cheese. Cover and refrigerate. Meanwhile, whisk together salad dressing & seasoning mix, sour cream, lime juice, chili powder and taco sauce until smooth; refrigerate. Just before serving, arrange avocado slices on top and sprinkle with crushed tortilla chips. Toss with 1 cup (or more, if desired) prepared dressing and serve.

Splender o' Salads

Vegetable Potato Salad

Confetti Wild Rice Salad

Makes 8 side-dish servings

Prep Time: 20 minutes
Cook Time: 20 minutes
Chill Time: 1 hour

    1 package (6 ounces) white and wild rice mix
    1 *each* red and yellow bell pepper, seeded and chopped
    ¼ cup finely chopped red onion
    ¼ cup minced fresh parsley
    ¼ cup minced fresh basil leaves
    ⅓ cup *French's®* Napa Valley Style Dijon Mustard
    ¼ cup olive oil
    ¼ cup red wine vinegar

Prepare rice according to package directions; cool completely.

Place rice in large bowl. Add peppers, onion, parsley and basil. Combine mustard, oil and vinegar in small bowl; mix well. Pour over rice and vegetables; toss well to coat evenly. Cover and refrigerate 1 hour before serving. Garnish as desired.

Pineapple Chicken Salad

Makes 4 to 6 servings

    1 packet (1 ounce) HIDDEN VALLEY® The Original Ranch® Salad Dressing
        & Seasoning Mix
    ½ cup mayonnaise
    1 can (20 ounces) pineapple chunks, reserving ¼ cup juice
    2 cups cubed, cooked chicken
    1 cup sliced celery

Combine dressing mix with mayonnaise and reserved ¼ cup pineapple juice. Add chicken, celery and pineapple chunks to mixture and toss well to coat. Chill.

Confetti Wild Rice Salad

Melon Salad

Makes 10 servings

Preparation Time: 15 minutes
Refrigerating Time: 5½ hours

2½ cups boiling apple juice
  1 package (8-serving size) *or* 2 packages (4-serving size each) JELL-O®
      Brand Watermelon Flavor Gelatin Dessert or JELL-O® Brand
      Watermelon Flavor Sugar Free Low Calorie Gelatin Dessert
1½ cups cold seltzer or club soda
  1 teaspoon lemon juice
  2 cups cantaloupe and honeydew melon cubes

STIR boiling juice into gelatin in large bowl at least 2 minutes until completely dissolved. Stir in cold seltzer and lemon juice. Refrigerate about 1½ hours or until thickened (spoon drawn through leaves definite impression). Stir in melon cubes. Spoon into 6-cup mold.

REFRIGERATE 4 hours or until firm. Unmold. Garnish as desired.

Oriental Turkey Noodle Salad

82

Makes 4 servings

  ½ teaspoon sesame oil
  ½ teaspoon reduced-sodium soy sauce
  1 package (3 ounces) chicken flavor instant oriental noodle soup mix,
      prepared according to package directions
  ¾ pound fully-cooked oven-roasted turkey breast, cut into ¼-inch cubes
  4 ounces water chestnuts, drained and sliced
  2 ounces fresh snow peas, blanched*
  2 large fresh mushrooms, sliced
  ½ cup diagonally cut carrots
  2 tablespoons sliced green onion

*To blanch snow peas: Plunge pea pods in boiling water 45 seconds. Immediately drain and plunge into ice water.

1. In small bowl, combine sesame oil, soy sauce and prepared soup mix. Cover and refrigerate.

2. In large bowl, combine turkey, water chestnuts, peas, mushrooms, carrots and green onions. Fold noodle mixture into turkey mixture. Cover and refrigerate 2 hours.

Favorite recipe from **National Turkey Federation**

Melon Salad

One-Dish Extravaganza

Peanut Chicken Stir-Fry

Makes 4 servings

> 1 package (6.1 ounces) RICE-A-RONI® With ⅓ Less Salt Fried Rice
> ½ cup reduced-sodium or regular chicken broth
> 2 tablespoons creamy peanut butter
> 1 tablespoon reduced-sodium or regular soy sauce
> 1 tablespoon vegetable oil
> ¾ pound skinless, boneless chicken breasts, cut into ½-inch pieces
> 2 cloves garlic, minced
> 2 cups frozen mixed carrots, broccoli and red pepper vegetable medley, thawed, drained
> 2 tablespoons chopped peanuts (optional)

1. Prepare Rice-A-Roni® mix as package directs.

2. While Rice-A-Roni® is simmering, combine chicken broth, peanut butter and soy sauce; mix with fork. Set aside.

3. In second large skillet or wok, heat oil over medium-high heat. Stir-fry chicken and garlic 2 minutes.

4. Add vegetables and broth mixture; stir-fry 5 to 7 minutes or until sauce has thickened. Serve over rice. Sprinkle with peanuts, if desired.

Peanut Chicken Stir-Fry

Turkey Cottage Pie

Makes about 8 servings

¼ **cup butter or margarine**
¼ **cup all-purpose flour**
1 **envelope LIPTON® RECIPE SECRETS® Golden Onion Soup Mix**
2 **cups water**
2 **cups cut-up cooked turkey or chicken**
1 **package (10 ounces) frozen mixed vegetables, thawed**
1¼ **cups shredded Swiss cheese (about 5 ounces), divided**
⅛ **teaspoon pepper**
5 **cups hot mashed potatoes**

Preheat oven to 375°F.

In large saucepan, melt butter and add flour; cook, stirring constantly, 5 minutes or until golden. Stir in golden onion soup mix thoroughly blended with water. Bring to a boil, then simmer 15 minutes or until thickened. Stir in turkey, vegetables, 1 cup cheese and pepper. Turn into lightly greased 2-quart casserole; top with hot potatoes, then remaining ¼ cup cheese. Bake 30 minutes or until bubbling.

Microwave Directions: In 2-quart casserole, heat butter at HIGH (100% power) 1 minute. Stir in flour and heat uncovered, stirring frequently, 2 minutes. Stir in golden onion soup mix thoroughly blended with water. Heat uncovered, stirring occasionally, 4 minutes or until thickened. Stir in turkey, vegetables, 1 cup cheese and pepper. Top with hot potatoes, then remaining ¼ cup cheese. Heat uncovered, turning casserole occasionally, 5 minutes or until bubbling. Let stand uncovered 5 minutes. For additional color, sprinkle, if desired, with paprika.

One-Dish Extravaganza

Turkey Cottage Pie

Mexicali Cornbread Casserole

Makes 4 servings

2½ cups frozen mixed vegetables, thawed
1½ cups cubed HILLSHIRE FARM® Ham
1 package (10 ounces) cornbread stuffing mix
2 cups milk
3 eggs, lightly beaten
Salt and black pepper to taste
½ cup (2 ounces) shredded taco-flavored cheese

Preheat oven to 375°F.

Combine mixed vegetables, Ham and stuffing mix in small casserole; set aside. Combine milk, eggs, salt and pepper in medium bowl; pour over ham mixture. Bake, covered, 45 minutes. Top with cheese; bake, uncovered, 3 minutes or until cheese is melted.

Southwestern Chicken Skillet

Makes 4 servings

Prep Time: 20 minutes

1½ cups water
1 package KNORR® Recipe Classics™ Tomato with Basil Soup, Dip and
    Recipe Mix
1 to 2 teaspoons chili powder
1 tablespoon MAZOLA® oil
1 pound boneless, skinless chicken breasts, cut into 1-inch chunks
1 can (14 ounces) creamed, Mexican or whole kernel corn
1 bag (12 ounces) tortilla chips or corn bread

• In small bowl, combine water, recipe mix and chili powder; set aside.

• In 10-inch skillet, heat oil over medium-high heat; add chicken and sauté 3 to 5 minutes or until lightly browned. Stir in recipe mixture and corn and bring to a boil; reduce heat and simmer 5 minutes.

• Serve with tortilla chips or cornbread.

One-Dish Extravaganza

Mexicali Cornbread Casserole

Easy Beef Stroganoff

Makes 4 to 6 servings

> 3 cans (10¾ ounces each) condensed cream of chicken soup or condensed cream of mushroom soup, undiluted
> 1 cup sour cream
> ½ cup water
> 1 envelope (1 ounce) dried onion soup mix
> 2 pounds cubed beef stew meat

Slow Cooker Directions

Combine soup, sour cream, water and onion soup mix in slow cooker. Add beef; stir until well coated. Cover and cook on HIGH 3 hours or on LOW 6 hours. Serve over hot cooked wild rice or noodles.

Savory Lo Mein

Makes about 4 servings

> 2 tablespoons olive or vegetable oil
> 1 medium clove garlic, finely chopped*
> 1 small head bok choy, cut into 2-inch pieces (about 5 cups)**
> 1 envelope LIPTON® RECIPE SECRETS® Onion Soup Mix***
> 1 cup water
> 2 tablespoons sherry (optional)
> 1 teaspoon soy sauce
> ¼ teaspoon ground ginger (optional)
> 8 ounces linguine or spaghetti, cooked and drained

*If using LIPTON® Recipe Secrets® Savory Herb with Garlic Soup Mix, omit garlic.

**Or use 5 cups coarsely shredded green cabbage. Decrease 10-minute cook time to 3 minutes.

***Also terrific with LIPTON® RECIPE SECRETS® Onion-Mushroom, Savory Herb with Garlic, or Golden Onion Soup Mix.

In 12-inch skillet, heat oil over medium heat and cook garlic and bok choy, stirring frequently, 10 minutes or until crisp-tender. Stir in onion soup mix blended with water, sherry, soy sauce and ginger. Bring to a boil over high heat. Reduce heat to low and simmer uncovered, stirring occasionally, 5 minutes. Toss with hot linguine. Sprinkle, if desired, with toasted sesame seeds.

One-Dish Extravaganza

Easy Beef Stroganoff

Scalloped Chicken & Pasta

Makes 4 servings

    ¼ **cup margarine or butter, divided**
    1 **package (6.2 ounces) PASTA RONI® Shells & White Cheddar**
    2 **cups frozen mixed vegetables**
    ⅔ **cup milk**
    2 **cups chopped cooked chicken or ham**
    ¼ **cup dry bread crumbs**

1. Preheat oven to 450°F.

2. In 3-quart saucepan, combine 2¼ cups water and 2 tablespoons margarine. Bring just to a boil. Stir in pasta and frozen vegetables. Reduce heat to medium.

3. Boil, uncovered, stirring frequently, 12 to 14 minutes or until most of water is absorbed. Add Special Seasonings, milk and chicken. Continue cooking 3 minutes.

4. Meanwhile, melt remaining 2 tablespoons margarine in small saucepan; stir in bread crumbs.

5. Transfer pasta mixture to 8- or 9-inch glass baking dish. Sprinkle with bread crumbs. Bake 10 minutes or until bread crumbs are browned and edges are bubbly.

Tuna and Rice Skillet Dinner

Makes 4 to 6 servings

Prep Time: 30 minutes

    1 **package (6½ ounces) chicken flavored rice mix**
    ½ **cup chopped onion**
      Water
  1½ **cups frozen peas and carrots, thawed**
    1 **can (10¾ ounces) cream of mushroom soup**
    ⅛ **teaspoon ground black pepper**
    1 **(7-ounce) pouch of STARKIST® Premium Albacore or Chunk Light Tuna**
    ⅓ **cup toasted slivered almonds (optional)**

In medium saucepan, combine rice mix and onion; add water according to package directions. Prepare rice according to package directions. Stir in vegetables, soup and pepper; blend well. Simmer, covered, 5 to 7 minutes, stirring occasionally. Stir in tuna; serve with almonds, if desired.

One-Dish Extravaganza

Scalloped Chicken & Pasta

Tamale Beef Pie

Makes 6 servings

Prep Time: 15 minutes
Cook Time: 26 minutes

  1½ **pounds ground beef**
    1 **package (1¼ ounces) taco seasoning mix**
    1 **can (11 ounces) whole kernel corn, drained**
    1 **can (10 ounces) tomatoes and green chilies**
    1 **cup chopped green or red bell peppers**
    3 **cups (6-ounce can)** *French's*® **French Fried Onions, divided**
    1 **package (8½ ounces) corn muffin mix**
  ½ **cup (2 ounces) shredded Cheddar cheese**

Preheat oven to 400°F. Brown ground beef in large nonstick skillet; drain. Stir in taco seasoning, corn, tomatoes and green chilies, bell peppers and *1½ cups* French Fried Onions. Pour mixture into 2-quart oblong baking dish.

Prepare corn muffin mix according to package directions. Spoon batter around edge of dish. Bake, uncovered, 20 minutes or until corn bread is golden. Top with cheese and remaining *1½ cups* onions. Bake, uncovered, 1 minute or until onions are golden.

Skillet Sausage and Peppers

Makes 4 servings

Prep Time: 15 minutes
Cook Time: 15 minutes

    1 **pound bulk Italian sausage**
    1 **medium onion, cut into wedges**
    1 **small green pepper, cut into strips**
    1 **small red pepper, cut into strips**
    1 **can (8 ounces) tomato sauce**
    1 **can (8 ounces) whole tomatoes, undrained**
  ½ **teaspoon dried oregano leaves**
    2 **cups STOVE TOP® Chicken Flavor Stuffing Mix in the Canister**

BROWN sausage in large skillet on medium-high heat. Stir in onion, peppers, tomato sauce, tomatoes and oregano. Bring to boil. Reduce heat to low; cover and simmer 5 minutes or until vegetables are tender-crisp.

STIR in Stuffing Mix Pouch just to moisten; cover. Remove from heat. Let stand 5 minutes.

One-Dish Extravaganza

Chinese Pork & Vegetable Stir-Fry

Makes about 4 servings

- **2 tablespoons vegetable oil, divided**
- **1 pound pork tenderloin or boneless beef sirloin, cut into ¼-inch slices**
- **6 cups assorted fresh vegetables***
- **1 can (8 ounces) sliced water chestnuts, drained**
- **1 envelope LIPTON® Recipe Secrets® Onion Soup Mix**
- **¾ cup water**
- **½ cup orange juice**
- **1 tablespoon soy sauce**
- **¼ teaspoon garlic powder**

*Use any of the following to equal 6 cups: broccoli florets, snow peas, thinly sliced red or green bell peppers and thinly sliced carrots.

In 12-inch skillet, heat 1 tablespoon oil over medium-high heat; brown pork. Remove and set aside.

In same skillet, heat remaining 1 tablespoon oil and cook assorted fresh vegetables, stirring occasionally, 5 minutes. Stir in water chestnuts and onion soup mix blended with water, orange juice, soy sauce and garlic powder. Bring to a boil over high heat. Reduce heat to low and simmer, uncovered, 3 minutes. Return pork to skillet and cook 1 minute or until heated through.

Southwest Stir-Fry

Makes 4 servings

- **1 bag SUCCESS® Rice**
- **1 pound ground turkey**
- **1 medium onion, chopped**
- **1 package (1.7 ounces) taco seasoning mix**
- **1 can (15¼ ounces) kidney beans, drained**
- **1 can (8 ounces) Mexican-style corn, drained**
- **½ cup fat-free sour cream**

Prepare rice according to package directions.

Brown ground turkey with onion in large skillet, stirring occasionally to separate turkey; drain. Stir in taco seasoning. Add rice, beans and corn; heat thoroughly, stirring occasionally. Stir in sour cream.

One-Dish Extravaganza

Country French Chicken Breasts

Makes about 4 servings

- **1 tablespoon I CAN'T BELIEVE IT'S NOT BUTTER!® Spread**
- **1 pound boneless, skinless chicken breast halves**
- **1 envelope LIPTON® RECIPE SECRETS® Savory Herb with Garlic or Golden Onion Soup Mix**
- **1 cup water**
- **1 tablespoon lemon juice**
- **Hot cooked rice**
- **4 lemon slices (optional)**

In 12-inch skillet, melt I Can't Believe It's Not Butter!® Spread over medium-high heat and brown chicken. Stir in soup mix blended with water and lemon juice. Reduce heat to low and simmer covered 10 minutes or until sauce is slightly thickened and chicken is no longer pink. To serve, arrange chicken over hot rice and spoon sauce over chicken. Garnish, if desired, with lemon slices.

Rice and Veggie Cheese Medley

Makes 4 servings

- **2 tablespoons butter or margarine**
- **1 small onion, chopped**
- **¾ teaspoon Italian herb seasoning, crushed**
- **1 package (10 ounces) frozen mixed vegetables**
- **1 box UNCLE BEN'S® COUNTRY INN® Three Cheese Rice**
- **1 cup water**
- **1 cup milk**
- **¾ cup (3 ounces) shredded pizza cheese blend**

1. Melt butter in large skillet over medium-high heat. Add onion and herb seasoning. Cook 3 minutes or until onion is soft.

2. Add vegetables and rice, reserving seasoning packet; cook 2 minutes. Add water, milk and contents of seasoning packet. Bring to a boil. Cover; reduce heat and simmer 10 minutes, stirring occasionally. Remove from heat.

3. Let stand, covered, 5 minutes. Stir in cheese.

One-Dish Extravaganza

Country French Chicken Breasts

Steaks with Peppers

Makes about 4 servings

>   2 tablespoons olive or vegetable oil
> 1½ pounds boneless beef chuck steaks, ½ inch thick (about 4 to 5)
>   2 medium red, green and/or yellow bell peppers, cut into thin strips
>   1 clove garlic, finely chopped (optional)
>   1 medium tomato, coarsely chopped
>   1 envelope LIPTON® RECIPE SECRETS® Onion or Onion-Mushroom Soup Mix
>   1 cup water

In 12-inch skillet, heat oil over medium-high heat and brown steaks. Remove steaks. Add peppers and garlic to skillet; cook over medium heat 5 minutes or until peppers are crisp-tender. Stir in tomato, then onion soup mix blended with water; bring to a boil over high heat. Reduce heat to low. Return steaks to skillet and simmer uncovered, stirring sauce occasionally, 25 minutes or until steaks and vegetables are tender.

Menu Suggestion: Serve with steak fries or baked potatoes.

Texas Ranch Chili Beans

Makes 8 servings

>   1 pound lean ground beef
>   1 can (28 ounces) whole peeled tomatoes, undrained
>   2 cans (15½ ounces each) chili beans
>   1 cup chopped onions
>   1 cup water
>   1 packet (1 ounce) HIDDEN VALLEY® The Original Ranch® Salad Dressing
>   & Seasoning Mix
>   1 teaspoon chili powder
>   1 bay leaf

In Dutch oven, brown beef over medium-high heat; drain off fat. Add tomatoes, breaking up with spoon. Stir in beans, onions, water, salad dressing & seasoning mix, chili powder and bay leaf. Bring to boil; reduce heat and simmer, uncovered, 1 hour, stirring occasionally. Remove bay leaf just before serving.

One-Dish Extravaganza

Steak with Peppers

Curried Chicken with Couscous

Makes 4 servings

Prep Time: 5 minutes
Cook Time: 15 minutes

> 1 package (5.7 ounces) curry flavor couscous mix
> 1 tablespoon butter or margarine
> 1 pound boneless skinless chicken breasts, cut into thin strips
> ½ bag (16 ounces) BIRDS EYE® frozen Farm Fresh Mixtures Broccoli,
>   Cauliflower & Red Peppers
> 1⅓ cups water
> ½ cup raisins

• Remove seasoning packet from couscous mix; set aside.

• In large nonstick skillet, melt butter over medium-high heat. Add chicken; cook until browned on all sides.

• Stir in vegetables, water, raisins and seasoning packet; bring to boil. Reduce heat to medium-low; cover and simmer 5 minutes or until chicken is no longer pink in center.

• Stir in couscous; cover. Remove from heat; let stand 5 minutes. Stir before serving. Garnish as desired.

Serving Suggestion: Serve with toasted pita bread rounds.

5-Minute Beef & Asparagus Stir-Fry

Makes 2 servings

> 1 box UNCLE BEN'S® Brown & Wild Rice Mushroom Recipe
> ¼ pound fresh asparagus, cut into 1-inch pieces
> 1 small onion, cut into wedges
> 1 medium red or yellow bell pepper, cut into strips
> 1 medium carrot, peeled and cut into thin diagonal slices
> ¼ pound deli roast beef sliced ¼ inch thick, cut into strips
> ⅓ cup purchased stir-fry sauce

1. Prepare rice according to package directions.

2. During the last 5 minutes of cooking, heat large nonstick skillet or wok over medium-high heat. Add remaining ingredients; simmer, stirring occasionally, until the vegetables are crisp-tender and the mixture is hot.

One-Dish Extravaganza

Curried Chicken with Couscous

Chicken and Pasta Primavera

Makes 6 servings

Prep Time: 20 minutes
Cook Time: 12 minutes

> 1 tablespoon margarine or butter
> ¾ pound boneless, skinless chicken breasts, cut into thin strips
> 2 cloves garlic, finely chopped
> 1 cup water
> ½ cup dry white wine or water
> 1 package KNORR® Recipe Classics™ Spring Vegetable Soup, Dip and Recipe Mix
> ½ teaspoon freshly ground pepper
> 8 ounces linguine, cooked and drained
> Grated Parmesan cheese (optional)

• In large skillet, melt margarine over medium-high heat and cook chicken and garlic, stirring frequently, 5 minutes.

• Stir in water, wine, recipe mix and pepper. Bring to a boil over high heat, stirring constantly. Reduce heat to low and simmer 5 minutes or until chicken is no longer pink in center.

102

• Toss chicken mixture with hot linguine. Serve, if desired, with grated cheese.

Helpful Hint

Thoroughly wash cutting surfaces, utensils and your hands with hot soapy water after handling uncooked chicken. This eliminates the risk of contaminating other foods with the salmonella bacteria that is often present in raw chicken. Salmonella is killed during cooking.

Chicken and Pasta Primavera

Fire Up the Grill!

Oriental Shrimp & Steak Kabobs
Makes about 8 servings

> 1 envelope LIPTON® RECIPE SECRETS® Savory Herb with Garlic
>   or Onion Soup Mix
> ¼ cup soy sauce
> ¼ cup lemon juice
> ¼ cup olive or vegetable oil
> ¼ cup honey
> ½ pound uncooked medium shrimp, peeled and deveined
> ½ pound boneless sirloin steak, cut into 1-inch cubes
> 16 cherry tomatoes
> 2 cups mushroom caps
> 1 medium green bell pepper, cut into chunks

In 13×9-inch glass baking dish, blend savory herb with garlic soup mix, soy sauce, lemon juice, oil and honey; set aside. On skewers, alternately thread shrimp, steak, tomatoes, mushrooms and green pepper. Add prepared skewers to baking dish; turn to coat. Cover and marinate in refrigerator, turning skewers occasionally, at least 2 hours. Remove prepared skewers, reserving marinade. Grill or broil, turning and basting frequently with reserved marinade, until shrimp turn pink and steak is cooked to desired doneness. Do not brush with marinade during last 5 minutes of cooking.

Menu Suggestion: Serve with corn-on-the-cob, a mixed green salad and grilled garlic bread.

Oriental Shrimp & Steak Kabobs

Tasty Taco Burgers

Makes 4 servings

1 pound ground beef
1 package (1¼ ounces) taco seasoning mix
8 KRAFT® American Singles Pasteurized Process Cheese Food
4 Kaiser rolls, split
  Lettuce leaves
  Salsa
  BREAKSTONE'S® or KNUDSEN® Sour Cream (optional)

MIX 1 pound ground beef and taco seasoning mix. Shape into 4 patties.

GRILL patties over hot coals 6 to 8 minutes on each side or to desired doneness. Top each patty with 2 process cheese food slices. Continue grilling until process cheese food is melted.

FILL rolls with lettuce and cheeseburgers. Top with salsa and sour cream, if desired.

Honey-Lime Pork Chops

Makes 4 servings

1 envelope LIPTON® RECIPE SECRETS® Savory Herb with Garlic Soup Mix*
⅓ cup soy sauce
3 tablespoons honey
3 tablespoons lime juice
1 teaspoon grated fresh ginger or ¼ teaspoon ground ginger (optional)
4 pork chops, 1½ inches thick

*Also terrific with LIPTON® RECIPE SECRETS® Garlic Mushroom or Onion Soup Mix.

1. For marinade, blend all ingredients except pork chops.

2. In shallow baking dish or plastic bag, pour ½ cup of the marinade over chops; turn to coat. Cover, or close bag, and marinate in refrigerator, turning occasionally, 2 to 24 hours. Refrigerate remaining marinade.

3. Remove chops from marinade, discarding marinade. Grill or broil chops, turning once and brushing with refrigerated marinade, until chops are done.

Fire Up the Grill!

Tasty Taco Burger

Grilled Vegetable Platter

Makes 6 servings

- **1 cup LAWRY'S® Herb & Garlic Marinade with Lemon Juice**
- **2 zucchini or yellow squash, cut into ½-inch-thick slices**
- **1 small onion, cut into wedges**
- **1 small Japanese eggplant, cut into ½-inch-thick slices**
- **2 red, green and/or yellow bell peppers, cut into chunks**
- **12 mushrooms, stems removed, or small portobello mushrooms, cut into ½-inch-thick slices**
- **Skewers**

In large resealable plastic food storage bag, combine all ingredients; mix well. Seal bag and marinate in refrigerator at least 30 minutes. Remove vegetables; reserve used marinade. Thread all vegetables except mushrooms onto skewers. Thread mushrooms onto separate skewers. Grill or broil mixed vegetable skewers 10 to 12 minutes or until tender, turning once and basting often with reserved marinade. Add mushroom skewers during final 2 minutes of grilling.

Serving Suggestion: This is a great dish to take along to a picnic, to use for topping a main-dish salad or to wrap up in a tortilla and serve as a vegetarian sandwich.

Hint: May also be grilled using well-oiled grill basket.

Helpful Hint

If you're using wooden skewers, be sure to soak them in water before using them to prevent scorching.

Fire Up the Grill!

Grilled Vegetable Platter

Steakhouse London Broil

Makes 6 to 8 servings

Prep Time: 5 minutes
Marinate Time: 30 minutes to 3 hours
Grill Time: 20 minutes

> 1 package KNORR® Recipe Classics™ Roasted Garlic Herb or French Onion Soup, Dip and Recipe Mix
> ⅓ cup vegetable or olive oil
> 2 tablespoons red wine vinegar
> 1 (1½- to 2-pound) beef round steak (for London Broil) or flank steak

• In large plastic food bag or 13×9-inch glass baking dish, blend recipe mix, oil and vinegar.

• Add steak, turning to coat. Close bag, or cover, and marinate in refrigerator 30 minutes to 3 hours.

• Remove meat from marinade, discarding marinade. Grill or broil, turning occasionally, until desired doneness.

• Slice meat thinly across the grain.

Garlic Chicken: Substitute 6 to 8 boneless chicken breasts or 3 to 4 pounds bone-in chicken pieces for steak. Marinate as directed. Grill boneless chicken breasts 6 minutes or bone-in chicken pieces 20 minutes or until chicken is no longer pink in center.

Fire Up the Grill!

Steakhouse London Broil, Onion-Roasted Potatoes (page 160)

Lipton® Onion Burgers

Makes about 8 servings

Prep Time: 10 minutes
Cook Time: 12 minutes

1 envelope LIPTON® RECIPE SECRETS® Onion Soup Mix*
2 pounds ground beef
½ cup water

*Also terrific with LIPTON® RECIPE SECRETS® Beefy Onion, Onion-Mushroom, Beefy Mushroom, Savory Herb with Garlic or Ranch Soup Mix.

1. In large bowl, combine all ingredients; shape into 8 patties.

2. Grill or broil until done.

Mexicana Marinade Paste

Makes 4 servings

1 package (1.0 ounce) LAWRY'S® Taco Spices & Seasonings
1 tablespoon lime juice
1 tablespoon vegetable oil
4 boneless, skinless chicken breast halves (about 1 pound)

In small bowl, combine Taco Spices & Seasonings, lime juice and oil; mix well. Brush mixture onto both sides of chicken. Grill or broil chicken until no longer pink, about 10 to 15 minutes, turning halfway through grilling time.

Serving Suggestion: Serve with Mexican rice and black beans. Guacamole and chips would complement the meal, as well.

Hint: This paste can also be used on beef or pork.

Lipton® Onion Burgers

Grilled Swordfish Steaks

Makes 4 servings

1 cup uncooked UNCLE BEN'S® ORIGINAL CONVERTED® Brand Rice
4 (1-inch-thick) swordfish steaks (about 4 ounces each)
3 tablespoons Caribbean jerk seasoning
1 can (8 ounces) crushed pineapple in juice, drained
⅓ cup chopped macadamia nuts
1 tablespoon honey

1. Cook rice according to package directions.

2. During the last 10 minutes of cooking, coat both sides of swordfish steaks with jerk seasoning. Lightly spray grid of preheated grill with nonstick cooking spray. Grill swordfish over medium coals 10 to 12 minutes or until fish flakes easily when tested with fork, turning after 5 minutes.

3. Stir pineapple, nuts and honey into hot cooked rice; serve with fish.

Tip: For a nuttier flavor, macadamia nuts can be toasted. Place nuts in a small nonstick skillet and heat over medium-high heat about 5 minutes or until lightly browned, stirring occasionally.

Garden Garlic Burgers

Makes 6 servings

1½ pounds ground beef or turkey
1 envelope LIPTON® RECIPE SECRETS® Savory Herb with Garlic Soup Mix*
2 small carrots, finely shredded
1 small zucchini, shredded
1 egg, lightly beaten
¼ cup plain dry bread crumbs

Also terrific with LIPTON® RECIPE SECRETS® Onion or Onion-Mushroom Soup Mix.

1. In large bowl, combine all ingredients; shape into 6 patties.

2. Grill or broil until done. Serve, if desired, on hamburger buns or whole wheat rolls.

Fire Up the Grill!

Mission Ensenada Fish Tacos

Makes 6 servings

Prep Time: 15 minutes
Cook Time: 10 to 12 minutes

> 1 package (1.0 ounce) LAWRY'S® Chicken Taco Spices & Seasonings, divided
> ½ cup sour cream
> 2 to 3 tablespoons milk
> 1 tablespoon vegetable oil
> 1 tablespoon lime juice
> 1 pound cod or orange roughy fillets
> 6 flour tortillas (taco or fajita size), warmed to soften
> 2 cups shredded cabbage mix
> 1 can (2.25 ounces) sliced black olives, drained
> Fresh lime wedges

In small bowl, combine 2 teaspoons Chicken Taco Spices & Seasonings with sour cream and enough milk to thin to a pouring consistency; set aside. In another small bowl, combine remaining seasonings, oil and lime juice. Brush or spread seasoning paste over entire fish. Grill or broil until fish begins to flake easily, about 10 to 12 minutes. Evenly divide fish and place in center of each tortilla. Top with cabbage and reserved sauce. Garnish with olives and lime wedges.

Hint: Warmed corn tortillas may also be used.

Helpful Hint

To pan-fry: In medium skillet, heat a small amount of oil until hot. Carefully add fish and cook over medium heat 6 minutes. Turn fish and cook until fish begins to flake easily, 4 to 5 minutes.

115

Ranch-Style Fajitas

Makes 6 servings

> 2 pounds flank or skirt steak
> ½ cup vegetable oil
> ⅓ cup lime juice
> 2 packets (1 ounce each) HIDDEN VALLEY® The Original Ranch® Salad
>   Dressing & Seasoning Mix
> 1 teaspoon ground cumin
> ½ teaspoon black pepper
> 6 flour tortillas
>   Lettuce
>   Guacamole, prepared HIDDEN VALLEY® The Original Ranch® Dressing, and
>   picante sauce (for toppings)

Place steak in large baking dish. In small bowl, whisk together oil, lime juice, salad dressing & seasoning mix, cumin and pepper. Pour mixture over steak. Cover and refrigerate several hours or overnight.

Remove steak; place marinade in small saucepan. Bring to a boil. Grill steak over medium-hot coals 8 to 10 minutes or to desired doneness, turning once and basting with heated marinade during last 5 minutes of grilling. Remove steak and slice diagonally across grain into thin slices. Heat tortillas following package directions. Divide steak strips among tortillas; roll up to enclose. Serve with lettuce and desired toppings.

Helpful Hint

For food safety reasons, marinating meat or poultry during the last five minutes of grilling is not usually recommended. The marinade in this recipe, however, is boiled and isn't used again until the meat is nearly cooked. It can be safely applied to the meat during the last five minutes of grilling.

Fire Up the Grill!

Ranch-Style Fajitas

Fresco Marinated Chicken

Makes 4 servings

> 1 envelope LIPTON® RECIPE SECRETS® Savory Herb with Garlic Soup Mix*
> ⅓ cup water
> ¼ cup olive or vegetable oil
> 1 teaspoon lemon juice or vinegar
> 4 boneless, skinless chicken breast halves (about 1¼ pounds)

*Also terrific with LIPTON® RECIPE SECRETS® Golden Onion Soup Mix.

1. For marinade, blend all ingredients except chicken.

2. In shallow baking dish or plastic bag, pour ½ cup of the marinade over chicken. Cover, or close bag, and marinate in refrigerator, turning occasionally, up to 3 hours. Refrigerate remaining marinade.

3. Remove chicken, discarding marinade. Grill or broil chicken, turning once and brushing with refrigerated marinade until chicken is no longer pink.

Mississippi Barbecue Burgers

Makes 4 servings

Prep Time: 30 minutes
Grill Time: 10 to 15 minutes

> 1 cup FRANK'S® or SNOWFLOSS® Kraut, drained
> ⅓ cup cranberry sauce
> ¼ cup MISSISSIPPI® Barbecue Sauce
> 2 tablespoons brown sugar
> 1 egg, lightly beaten
> 1 envelope dried onion soup mix
> ¼ cup water
> 1 pound ground beef
> 4 onion or sesame seed hamburger rolls, split, lightly toasted

1. Mix kraut, cranberry sauce, barbecue sauce and brown sugar in small saucepan; bring to a boil. Reduce heat and simmer about 15 minutes, stirring occasionally.

2. Meanwhile, in medium bowl combine egg, soup mix and water. Let stand 5 minutes. Add ground beef; mix thoroughly. Form into 4 patties.

3. Barbecue patties over mesquite or charcoal to desired doneness. Serve on toasted rolls, topped with kraut mixture.

Fire Up the Grill!

Fresco Marinated Chicken

Charcoal Beef Kabobs

Makes 6 servings

½ cup vegetable oil
¼ cup lemon juice
1½ tablespoons (½ packet) HIDDEN VALLEY® The Original Ranch® Salad
    Dressing & Seasoning Mix
2 pounds beef top round or boneless sirloin steak, cut into
    1-inch cubes
1 or 2 red, yellow or green bell peppers, cut into 1-inch squares
16 pearl onions or 1 medium onion, cut into wedges
8 cherry tomatoes

Combine oil, lemon juice and dry salad dressing & seasoning mix. Pour over beef cubes in shallow dish. Cover and refrigerate 1 hour or longer. Drain beef; reserve marinade. Thread beef cubes, peppers and onions onto skewers. Grill kabobs on uncovered grill over medium-hot KINGSFORD® Briquets 15 minutes, brushing often with reserved marinade and turning to brown all sides. A few minutes before serving, add cherry tomatoes to ends of skewers.

Helpful Hint

Use a clean dish to hold the kabobs when they've finished grilling. Never use the same pan or platter, unless it's been cleaned, for both raw and uncooked foods.

Fire Up the Grill!

Cheesy Spinach Burgers

Makes 8 servings

> 1 envelope LIPTON® RECIPE SECRETS® Onion Soup Mix
> 2 pounds ground beef
> 1 package (10 ounces) frozen chopped spinach, thawed and squeezed dry
> 1 cup shredded mozzarella or Cheddar cheese (about 4 ounces)

1. In large bowl, combine all ingredients; shape into 8 patties.

2. Grill or broil until done. Serve, if desired, on hamburger buns.

Southwest Paste

Makes 4 servings

> 1 package (1.0 ounce) LAWRY'S® Taco Spices & Seasonings
> ¼ cup LAWRY'S® Mesquite Marinade with Lime Juice
> 4 pounds baby back pork ribs

In small bowl, combine Taco Spices & Seasonings and Mesquite Marinade; mix well. Spread paste onto both sides of ribs. In large roasting pan, place ribs bone side down on wire rack. Bake in 300°F. oven 3 hours. Remove from oven. Grill over low heat additional 20 to 25 minutes or until tender.

Serving Suggestion: Serve with warm tortillas and honey butter.

Cheesy Spinach Burger

All-Time Favorites

Country French Chicken Skillet
Makes 4 to 6 servings

Prep Time: 5 minutes
Cook Time: 16 minutes

    2 **tablespoons margarine or butter**
1½ **pounds boneless, skinless chicken breast halves**
    1 **cup water**
    1 **package KNORR® Recipe Classics™ Vegetable or Spring Vegetable Soup, Dip and Recipe Mix**
  ¼ **teaspoon dried dill weed (optional)**
  ½ **cup sour cream**

• In large skillet, melt margarine over medium-high heat and brown chicken, turning occasionally, 5 minutes.

• Stir in water, recipe mix and dill weed. Bring to a boil over high heat. Reduce heat to low and simmer covered, stirring occasionally, 10 minutes or until chicken is no longer pink. Remove only chicken to serving platter; keep warm.

• Remove skillet from heat; stir in sour cream. Spoon sauce over chicken and serve, if desired, with noodles.

Country French Chicken Skillet

Skillet Beef & Broccoli

Makes 4 servings

Prep Time: 10 minutes
Cook Time: 15 minutes

> 1 tablespoon olive or vegetable oil
> 1 pound sirloin steak, cut into 1-inch strips
> 1 package (10 ounces) frozen broccoli florets, thawed
> 1 envelope LIPTON® RECIPE SECRETS® Onion Soup Mix*
> 1¼ cups water
> 1 tablespoon firmly packed brown sugar
> 1 tablespoon soy sauce

*Also terrific with LIPTON® RECIPE SECRETS® Onion-Mushroom Soup Mix.

1. In 12-inch nonstick skillet, heat oil over medium-high heat and brown steak, stirring occasionally, in two batches. Remove steak from skillet and set aside.

2. Stir in broccoli and soup mix blended with water, brown sugar and soy sauce. Bring to a boil over high heat. Reduce heat to low and simmer uncovered, stirring occasionally, 2 minutes.

3. Return steak to skillet and cook 1 minute or until steak is done. Serve, if desired, with hot cooked rice.

Simple Stir-Fry

Makes 4 servings

> 1 tablespoon vegetable oil
> 12 boneless, skinless chicken tenderloins, cut into 1-inch pieces
> 1 bag (1 pound) frozen stir-fry vegetable mix
> 2 tablespoons soy sauce
> 2 tablespoons honey
> 2 (2-cup) bags UNCLE BEN'S® Boil-in-Bag Rice

1. Heat oil in large skillet or wok. Add chicken; cook over medium-high heat 6 to 8 minutes or until lightly browned. Add vegetables, soy sauce and honey. Cover and cook 5 to 8 minutes or until chicken is no longer pink in center and vegetables are crisp-tender.

2. Meanwhile, cook rice according to package directions. Serve stir-fry over rice.

All-Time Favorites

Skillet Beef & Broccoli

Tamale Pie

Makes 6 servings

Prep and Cook Time: 20 minutes

> 1 pound ground round
> 1 package (10 ounces) frozen corn, thawed
> 1 can (14½ ounces) diced tomatoes, undrained
> 1 can (4 ounces) sliced black olives, drained
> 1 package (1¼ ounces) taco seasoning mix
> 1 package (6 ounces) corn muffin or corn bread mix plus ingredients to
>   prepare mix
> ¼ cup (1 ounce) shredded Cheddar cheese
> 1 green onion, thinly sliced

1. Preheat oven to 400°F. Place meat in large skillet; cook over high heat 6 to 8 minutes or until meat is no longer pink, breaking meat apart with wooden spoon. Pour off drippings. Add corn, tomatoes, olives and seasoning mix to meat. Bring to a boil over medium-high heat, stirring constantly. Pour into deep 9-inch pie plate; smooth top with spatula.

2. Prepare corn muffin mix according to package directions. Spread evenly over meat mixture. Bake 8 to 10 minutes or until golden brown. Sprinkle with cheese and onion slices. Let stand 10 minutes before serving.

Serving Suggestion: Serve with papaya wedges sprinkled with lime juice.

Tamale Pie

Quick Chicken Stir-Fry

Makes 6 servings

Prep Time: 10 minutes
Cook Time: 12 minutes

> **4 TYSON® Fresh Boneless, Skinless Chicken Breasts**
> **6 cups cooked UNCLE BEN'S® NATURAL SELECT™ Chicken & Herb Rice**
> **1 clove garlic, minced**
> **1 package (10 ounces) frozen broccoli, green beans, mushrooms and red peppers**
> **1 medium onion, cut into wedges**
> **⅓ cup shredded carrots**
> **½ cup bottled hoisin sauce**

PREP: CLEAN: Wash hands. Cut chicken into ¾-inch pieces. CLEAN: Wash hands.

COOK: Spray large nonstick skillet with nonstick cooking spray. Heat over medium-high heat. Add chicken and garlic; stir-fry 4 minutes. Add frozen vegetables, onion and carrots; stir-fry 3 minutes. Cover; cook 3 to 5 minutes or until vegetables are tender and internal juices of chicken run clear. (Or insert instant-read meat thermometer into thickest part of chicken. Temperature should read 170°F.) Stir in hoisin sauce. Heat thoroughly.

SERVE: Serve chicken and vegetables over hot cooked rice. Garnish with fresh cilantro, if desired.

CHILL: Refrigerate leftovers immediately.

Quick Chicken Stir-Fry

Mama's Best Ever Spaghetti & Meatballs

Makes 4 servings

Prep Time: 10 minutes
Cook Time: 20 minutes

> **1 pound lean ground beef**
> **½ cup Italian seasoned dry bread crumbs**
> **1 egg**
> **1 jar (26 to 28 ounces) RAGÚ® Old World Style® Pasta Sauce**
> **8 ounces spaghetti, cooked and drained**

1. In medium bowl, combine ground beef, bread crumbs and egg; shape into 12 meatballs.

2. In 3-quart saucepan, bring Ragú Pasta Sauce to a boil over medium-high heat. Gently stir in meatballs.

3. Reduce heat to low and simmer covered, stirring occasionally, 20 minutes or until meatballs are no longer pink in center. Serve over hot spaghetti; sprinkle with shredded Parmesan cheese if desired.

Lemon-Twist Chicken

Makes about 4 servings

> **2 tablespoons olive or vegetable oil**
> **4 boneless, skinless chicken breast halves (about 1¼ pounds)**
> **1 envelope LIPTON® RECIPE SECRETS® Savory Herb with Garlic Soup Mix***
> **1¼ cups water**
> **2 tablespoons lemon juice**
> **1 tablespoon honey**
> **1 teaspoon soy sauce**

*Also terrific with LIPTON® RECIPE SECRETS® Golden Onion Soup Mix.

In 12-inch skillet, heat oil over medium-high heat and brown chicken. Stir in savory herb with garlic soup mix blended with water, lemon juice, honey and soy sauce. Bring to a boil over high heat. Reduce heat to low and simmer uncovered 10 minutes or until chicken is done. Serve, if desired, over hot cooked noodles or rice.

All-Time Favorites

Mama's Best Ever Spaghetti & Meatballs

Classic Chicken Biscuit Pie

Makes 8 to 10 servings

12 boneless, skinless chicken tenderloins, cut into 1-inch pieces
4 cups water
2 boxes UNCLE BEN'S® COUNTRY INN® Chicken Flavored Rice
1 can (10¾ ounces) condensed cream of chicken soup
1 bag (1 pound) frozen peas, potatoes and carrots
1 container (12 ounces) refrigerated buttermilk biscuits

1. Heat oven to 400°F. In large saucepan, combine chicken, water, rice, contents of seasoning packets, soup and vegetable mixture; mix well. Bring to a boil. Cover; reduce heat and simmer 10 minutes.

2. Place in 13×9-inch baking pan; top with biscuits.

3. Bake 10 to 12 minutes or until biscuits are golden brown.

Tip: For individual pot pies, place rice mixture in small ramekins or casseroles. Proceed with recipe as directed.

Turkey Tetrazzini

Makes 4 servings

Prep Time: 20 minutes
Cook Time: 20 minutes

8 ounces uncooked spaghetti
1½ cups diced cooked turkey
2 cups water
½ cup HELLMANN'S® or BEST FOODS® Mayonnaise
1 package KNORR® Recipe Classics™ Leek Soup, Dip and Recipe Mix
½ cup frozen peas
1 jar (6 ounces) sliced mushrooms, drained
⅓ cup grated Parmesan cheese

• Preheat oven to 375°F.

• Cook spaghetti according to package directions; drain. In same pot, stir turkey, water, mayonnaise, recipe mix, peas and mushrooms until blended.

• Add spaghetti; toss to combine. Spoon into 2-quart baking dish. Cover with foil.

• Bake 20 minutes. Uncover and sprinkle with Parmesan cheese. Bake 5 minutes longer or until hot and bubbly.

All-Time Favorites

Foolproof Clam Fettuccine

Makes 4 servings

- **1 package (6 ounces) fettucine-style noodles with creamy cheese sauce mix**
- **¾ cup milk**
- **1 can (6½ ounces) chopped clams, undrained**
- **¼ cup (1 ounce) grated Parmesan cheese**
- **1 teaspoon parsley flakes**
- **1 can (4 ounces) mushroom stems and pieces, drained**
- **2 tablespoons diced pimiento**
- **1⅓ cups *French's*® French Fried Onions, divided**

Preheat oven to 375°F. In large saucepan, cook noodles according to package directions; drain. Return hot noodles to saucepan; stir in sauce mix, milk, undrained clams, Parmesan cheese, parsley flakes, mushrooms, pimiento and ⅔ *cup* French Fried Onions. Heat and stir 3 minutes or until bubbly. Pour into 10×6-inch baking dish. Bake, covered, at 375°F for 30 minutes or until thickened. Place remaining ⅔ *cup* onions around edges of casserole; bake, uncovered, 3 minutes or until onions are golden brown.

Helpful Hint

You can make this dish in your microwave, too. First, prepare the noodle mixture as directed in the recipe, and pour it into a 10×6-inch microwave-safe dish. Cook, covered, on HIGH 4 to 6 minutes or until heated through, stirring halfway through the cooking time. Top with the remaining ⅔ cup onions as directed. Cook, uncovered, 1 minute. Let stand 5 minutes before serving.

Cajun Chicken Bayou

Makes 2 servings

2 cups water
1 can (10 ounces) diced tomatoes and green chilies, undrained
1 box UNCLE BEN'S® CHEF'S RECIPE™ Traditional Red Beans & Rice
2 boneless, skinless chicken breasts (about 8 ounces)

1. In large skillet, combine water, tomatoes, beans & rice and contents of seasoning packet; mix well.

2. Add chicken. Bring to a boil. Cover; reduce heat and simmer 20 minutes or until chicken is no longer pink in center.

Hint: If you prefer a spicier dish, add hot pepper sauce just before serving.

Souper Quick "Lasagna"

Makes about 6 servings

1½ pounds ground beef
1 envelope LIPTON® RECIPE SECRETS® Onion or Onion-Mushroom Soup Mix
3 cans (8 ounces each) tomato sauce
1 cup water
½ teaspoon dried oregano leaves (optional)
1 package (8 ounces) broad egg noodles, cooked and drained
1 package (16 ounces) mozzarella cheese, shredded

Preheat oven to 375°F.

In 12-inch skillet, brown ground beef over medium-high heat; drain. Stir in onion soup mix, tomato sauce, water and oregano. Simmer covered, stirring occasionally, 15 minutes.

In 2-quart oblong baking dish, spoon enough ground beef mixture to cover bottom. Alternately layer noodles, ground beef mixture and cheese, ending with cheese. Bake 30 minutes or until bubbling.

Microwave Directions: In 2-quart casserole, microwave ground beef, uncovered, at HIGH (Full Power) 7 minutes, stirring once; drain. Stir in onion soup mix, tomato sauce, water and oregano. Microwave at MEDIUM (50% Power) 5 minutes, stirring once. In 2-quart oblong microwavable dish, spoon enough of mixture to cover bottom. Alternately layer as above. Microwave covered at MEDIUM, turning dish occasionally, 10 minutes or until bubbling. Let stand covered 5 minutes.

136

Cajun Chicken Bayou

Easy Pasta Bake with Vegetables

Makes 6 servings

>   1 package (16 ounces) frozen mixed vegetables, thawed
>   5 cups cooked pasta
>   1 jar (28 ounces) reduced calorie pasta sauce
>   ½ cup KRAFT FREE® Nonfat Grated Topping
>   1 package (8 ounces) KRAFT® 2% Reduced Fat Milk Shredded
>   Low-Moisture Part Skim Mozzarella Cheese

STIR vegetables, pasta, sauce and grated topping together.

SPOON into 13×9-inch baking dish. Top with mozzarella cheese.

BAKE at 375°F for 20 minutes.

Pork Chops Piquante

Makes about 4 servings

>   2 teaspoons olive or vegetable oil, divided
>   4 pork chops, ¾ inch thick
>   1 medium onion, thinly sliced
>   1½ teaspoons ketchup
>   ½ cup dry white wine
>   1 envelope LIPTON® RECIPE SECRETS® Savory Herb with Garlic Soup Mix
>   1¼ cups water
>   2 tablespoons finely sliced sweet gherkin pickles

In 12-inch skillet, heat 1 teaspoon oil over medium-high heat and brown chops; remove and set aside. In same skillet, heat remaining 1 teaspoon oil over medium heat and brown onion. Add ketchup and cook over medium heat, stirring frequently, 1 minute. Add wine and boil over high heat 1 minute. Stir in savory herb with garlic soup mix blended with water. Bring to a boil over high heat; reduce heat to low. Return pork chops to skillet and simmer covered 10 minutes. Add pickles and continue simmering 5 minutes or until pork is done.

Serving Suggestion: Serve with baked potatoes and applesauce.

Easy Pasta Bake with Vegetables

Broccoli, Chicken and Rice Casserole
Makes 4 servings

> **1 box** UNCLE BEN'S CHEF'S RECIPE™ Broccoli Rice Au Gratin Supreme
> **2 cups** boiling water
> **4** boneless, skinless chicken breasts (about 1 pound)
> **¼ teaspoon** garlic powder
> **2 cups** frozen broccoli
> **1 cup** (4 ounces) reduced-fat shredded Cheddar cheese

1. Heat oven to 425°F. In 13×9-inch baking pan, combine rice and contents of seasoning packet. Add boiling water; mix well. Add chicken; sprinkle with garlic powder. Cover and bake 30 minutes.

2. Add broccoli and cheese; continue to bake, covered, 8 to 10 minutes or until chicken is no longer pink in center.

Veggie Tuna Pasta
Makes 4 servings

Prep Time: 2 minutes
Cook Time: 12 to 15 minutes

> **1 package** (16 ounces) medium pasta shells
> **1 bag** (16 ounces) BIRDS EYE® frozen Farm Fresh Mixtures Broccoli, Corn & Red Peppers
> **1 can** (10 ounces) chunky light tuna, packed in water
> **1 can** (10¾ ounces) reduced-fat cream of mushroom soup

• In large saucepan, cook pasta according to package directions. Add vegetables during last 10 minutes; drain and return to saucepan.

• Stir in tuna and soup. Add salt and pepper to taste. Cook over medium heat until heated through.

Variation: Stir in 1 can (4 to 6 ounces) chopped ripe olives with tuna.

Serving Suggestion: For a creamier dish, add a few tablespoons water with soup; blend well.

All-Time Favorites

Broccoli, Chicken and Rice Casserole

Harvest Pot Roast with Sweet Potatoes

Makes 6 servings

- **1 envelope LIPTON® RECIPE SECRETS® Onion Soup Mix**
- **1½ cups water**
- **¼ cup soy sauce**
- **2 tablespoons firmly packed dark brown sugar**
- **1 teaspoon ground ginger (optional)**
- **1 (3- to 3½-pound) boneless pot roast (rump, chuck or round)**
- **4 large sweet potatoes, peeled, if desired, and cut into large chunks**
- **3 tablespoons water**
- **2 tablespoons all-purpose flour**

1. Preheat oven to 325°F. In Dutch oven or 5-quart heavy ovenproof saucepot, combine soup mix, water, soy sauce, brown sugar and ginger; add roast.

2. Cover and bake 1 hour 45 minutes.

3. Add potatoes and bake covered an additional 45 minutes or until beef and potatoes are tender.

4. Remove roast and potatoes to serving platter and keep warm; reserve juices.

5. In small cup, with wire whisk, blend water and flour. In same Dutch oven, add flour mixture to reserved juices. Bring to a boil over high heat. Boil, stirring occasionally, 2 minutes. Serve with roast and potatoes.

142

Helpful Hint

While sweet potatoes and yams are two different vegetables, yams can be used in place of sweet potatoes in most recipes.

All-Time Favorites

Harvest Pot Roast with Sweet Potatoes

Catalina® Chicken Stir-Fry

Makes 4 to 6 servings

Prep Time: 10 minutes
Cook Time: 15 minutes

    2 cups MINUTE® White Rice, uncooked
    1 pound boneless skinless chicken breasts, cubed
    ¾ cup KRAFT® CATALINA® Dressing
    ¼ cup soy sauce
    ½ teaspoon garlic powder
    1 package (16 ounces) frozen mixed vegetables, thawed and drained, *or*
        3 cups cut-up fresh vegetables

PREPARE rice as directed on package.

COOK and stir chicken in dressing, soy sauce and garlic powder 5 minutes. Add vegetables; cover.

SIMMER 5 to 7 minutes or until vegetables are crisp-tender, stirring frequently. Serve over rice.

Chopped Beef Stroganoff

Makes about 4 servings

    1½ pounds ground beef
    1 small onion, chopped
    1 envelope LIPTON® RECIPE SECRETS® Beefy Mushroom Soup Mix
    2 tablespoons all-purpose flour
    2 cups water
    ½ cup sour cream
        Hot cooked noodles (optional)

In 12-inch skillet, brown ground beef with onion over medium-high heat until onion is tender. Stir in soup mix, flour and water. Bring to a boil over high heat. Reduce heat to low. Cover and simmer 10 minutes. Stir in sour cream; heat through. Do not boil. Serve over hot noodles.

All-Time Favorites

Catalina® Chicken Stir-Fry

Sides of All Kinds

Vegetables & Wild Rice
Makes 6 servings

Prep Time: none
Cook Time: 30 minutes

1 box UNCLE BEN'S® Long Grain & Wild Rice Roasted Garlic
2⅓ cups water
2 tablespoons butter or margarine
1 cup corn, fresh or frozen
1 medium tomato, chopped
4 strips bacon, cooked and crumbled
3 tablespoons chopped green onions

COOK: CLEAN: Wash hands. In medium skillet, combine water, butter, rice and contents of seasoning packet. Bring to a boil. Cover tightly and simmer 15 minutes. Add corn and simmer 15 minutes or until water is absorbed. Stir in tomato and bacon. Sprinkle with green onions.

SERVE: Serve with garlic toast, if desired.

CHILL: Refrigerate leftovers immediately.

Vegetables & Wild Rice

Savory Skillet Broccoli

Makes 4 servings

Prep Time: 5 minutes
Cook Time: 10 minutes

    1 tablespoon olive or vegetable oil
    6 cups fresh broccoli florets *or* 1 pound green beans, trimmed
    1 envelope LIPTON® RECIPE SECRETS® Golden Onion Soup Mix*
1½ cups water

*Also terrific with LIPTON® RECIPE SECRETS® Onion-Mushroom Soup Mix.

1. In 12-inch skillet, heat oil over medium-high heat and cook broccoli, stirring occasionally, 2 minutes.

2. Stir in soup mix blended with water. Bring to a boil over high heat.

3. Reduce heat to medium-low and simmer covered 6 minutes or until broccoli is tender.

Hash Brown Bake

Makes 4 servings

148

    1 packet (1 ounce) HIDDEN VALLEY® The Original Ranch® Salad Dressing
        & Seasoning Mix
1¼ cups milk
    3 ounces cream cheese
    6 cups hash browns, frozen shredded potatoes
    1 tablespoon bacon bits
    ½ cup shredded sharp Cheddar cheese

In blender, combine salad dressing & seasoning mix, milk and cream cheese. Pour over potatoes and bacon bits in 9-inch baking dish. Top with cheese. Bake at 350°F for 35 minutes.

Savory Skillet Broccoli

Cornbread Stuffing with Sausage and Apple

Makes 4 servings

Prep and Cook Time: 20 minutes

⅓ cup pecan pieces
1 pound bulk pork sausage
1 large Jonathan apple
1⅓ cups chicken broth
¼ cup apple juice
6 ounces seasoned cornbread stuffing mix

1. Preheat oven to 300°F. Place nuts in shallow baking pan. Bake 6 to 8 minutes or until lightly browned, stirring frequently. Place sausage in large skillet; cook over high heat 10 minutes or until meat is no longer pink, breaking meat apart with wooden spoon. Pour off drippings.

2. Meanwhile, coarsely chop apple. Place in 3-quart saucepan. Add chicken broth, apple juice and seasoning packet from stuffing mix. Bring to a boil, uncovered, over high heat. Remove from heat and stir in stuffing mix. Cover and let stand 3 to 5 minutes or until stuffing is moist and tender. Stir sausage into stuffing. Spoon into serving bowl and top with nuts.

Fresh Vegetable Sauté

Makes 4 to 6 servings

Prep Time: 15 minutes
Cook Time: 15 minutes

2 tablespoons olive oil
6 cups assorted cut-up vegetables, such as broccoli flowerets, green beans, cauliflowerets, sugar snap peas, bell pepper strips, diagonally sliced carrots, mushrooms, onions, yellow squash and zucchini
1 envelope GOOD SEASONS® Italian Salad Dressing Mix
2 tablespoons red wine vinegar

HEAT oil in large skillet on medium-high heat. Add vegetables; cook and stir until tender-crisp.

ADD salad dressing mix and vinegar; cook and stir until heated through. Garnish with chopped fresh parsley, if desired.

Sides of All Kinds

Cornbread Stuffing with Sausage and Apple

Garlic Black Beans & Rice

Makes 4 servings

Prep Time: none
Cook Time: 15 minutes

> 2 cups UNCLE BEN'S NATURAL SELECT™ Chicken & Herb Rice
> 1 tablespoon olive oil
> ½ cup diced onion
> ½ cup diced green bell pepper
> 4 cloves garlic, minced
> 1 can (15 ounces) black beans, rinsed and drained
> 1 tablespoon fresh lime juice

COOK: CLEAN: Wash hands. In medium saucepan, heat oil until hot. Sauté onion, bell pepper and garlic 1 minute. Add rice and cook according to package directions. When rice has finished cooking, stir in beans and lime juice.

SERVE: Serve warm.

CHILL: Refrigerate leftovers immediately.

Hidden Valley® Glazed Baby Carrots

Makes 4 to 6 servings

> ¼ cup butter
> ¼ cup packed light brown sugar
> 1 package (16 ounces) ready-to-eat baby carrots, cooked
> 1 packet (1 ounce) HIDDEN VALLEY® The Original Ranch® Salad Dressing
>   & Seasoning Mix

Melt butter and sugar in a large skillet. Add carrots and salad dressing & seasoning mix; stir well. Cook over medium heat until carrots are tender and glazed, about 5 minutes, stirring frequently.

Sides of All Kinds

Garlic Black Beans & Rice

Garlic Mashed Potatoes

Makes 8 servings

> **6 medium all-purpose potatoes, peeled, if desired, and cut into chunks
>   (about 3 pounds)**
> **Water**
> **1 envelope LIPTON® RECIPE SECRETS® Garlic Mushroom Soup Mix***
> **½ cup milk**
> **½ cup margarine or butter, softened**

*Also terrific with LIPTON® RECIPE SECRETS® Savory Herb with Garlic, Onion or Golden Onion Soup Mix.

1. In 4-quart saucepan, cover potatoes with water; bring to a boil.

2. Reduce heat to low and simmer uncovered 20 minutes or until potatoes are very tender; drain.

3. Return potatoes to saucepan, then mash. Stir in remaining ingredients.

Oniony Corn Muffins

Makes 12 servings

Prep Time: 15 minutes
Bake Time: 15 minutes

> **1 package (12 ounces) corn muffin mix**
> **⅔ cup milk**
> **1 egg**
> **1 can (7 ounces) whole kernel corn, drained**
> **1⅓ cups *French's*® French Fried Onions, slightly crushed**

Preheat oven to 400°F. Grease 12-cup muffin pan. Prepare corn muffin mix according to package directions using milk and egg. Stir in corn and French Fried Onions. Do not overmix.

Fill muffin cups, using ¼ cup batter for each cup. Bake 15 minutes or until toothpick inserted into centers comes out clean. Cool in pan on wire rack 5 minutes. Loosen muffins from pan; remove and serve warm.

Sides of All Kinds

Garlic Mashed Potatoes

Italian Vegetables with Garlic Butter Rice

Makes 4 servings

Prep Time: 5 minutes
Cook Time: 15 minutes

> **1 package UNCLE BEN'S NATURAL SELECT™ Garlic & Butter Rice**
> **1 yellow squash, sliced**
> **1 zucchini, sliced**
> **1 cup diced red bell pepper**
> **1 cup sliced eggplant**
> **⅓ cup balsamic vinaigrette**
> **1 tablespoon chopped fresh rosemary**

PREP: CLEAN: Wash hands. In large bowl, combine vegetables, vinaigrette and rosemary; set aside 15 minutes.

COOK: Meanwhile, prepare rice according to package directions; set aside. Sauté vegetables in marinade until crisp-tender.

SERVE: Serve vegetable mixture over rice.

CHILL: Refrigerate leftovers immediately.

Helpful Hint

The western variety of eggplant is often salted before being cooked. This removes any bitterness, draws off moisture and reduces the amount of oil absorbed during cooking. Slice the eggplant and place the slices in a colander. Sprinkle the cut sides with salt. Allow the slices to drain 30 minutes; then rinse and pat them dry with paper towels. Another method of salting is to allow salted eggplant slices to stand between several sheets of paper towels weighted with a heavy plate for 30 minutes. Rinse, drain and pat the eggplant slices dry with paper towels before using them in the recipe.

Italian Vegetables with Garlic Butter Rice

Easy "Baked" Beans

Makes 6 servings

Prep Time: 10 minutes
Cook Time: 25 minutes

> 2 slices bacon, chopped
> 2 cans (19 ounces each) red kidney beans and/or cannellini beans, rinsed and drained
> 1 envelope LIPTON® RECIPE SECRETS® Beefy Onion Soup Mix
> 1½ cups water
> ¼ cup ketchup
> 2 tablespoons firmly packed brown sugar

1. In 3-quart saucepan, cook bacon over medium-high heat until crisp-tender. Stir in beans and continue cooking, stirring frequently, 1 minute.

2. Stir in remaining ingredients. Bring to a boil over high heat.

3. Reduce heat to medium-low and simmer uncovered 20 minutes or until thickened.

Bayou Dirty Rice

Makes 4 to 6 servings

Prep & Cook Time: 40 minutes

- ¼ **pound spicy sausage, crumbled**
- ½ **medium onion, chopped**
- 1 **stalk celery, sliced**
- 1 **package (6 ounces) wild and long grain rice seasoned mix**
- 1 **can (14½ ounces) DEL MONTE® Original Recipe Stewed Tomatoes**
- ½ **green pepper, chopped**
- ¼ **cup chopped parsley**

1. Brown sausage and onion in large skillet over medium-high heat; drain. Add celery, rice and rice seasoning packet; cook and stir 2 minutes.

2. Drain tomatoes, reserving liquid; pour liquid into measuring cup. Add water to measure 1⅓ cups; pour over rice. Add tomatoes; bring to boil. Cover and cook over low heat 20 minutes. Add pepper and parsley.

3. Cover and cook 5 minutes or until rice is tender. Serve with roasted chicken or Cornish game hens.

159

Creamy Broccoli and Cheese

Makes 4 servings

- 1 **package (8 ounces) cream cheese, softened**
- ¾ **cup milk**
- 1 **packet (1 ounce) HIDDEN VALLEY® The Original Ranch® Salad Dressing & Seasoning Mix**
- 1 **pound fresh broccoli, cooked and drained**
- ½ **cup (2 ounces) shredded sharp Cheddar cheese**

In a food processor fitted with a metal blade, blend cream cheese, milk and salad dressing & seasoning mix until smooth. Pour over broccoli in a 9-inch baking dish; stir well. Top with cheese. Bake at 350°F for 25 minutes or until cheese is melted.

Onion-Roasted Potatoes

Makes 4 servings

Prep Time: 10 minutes
Cook Time: 40 minutes

> **1 envelope LIPTON® RECIPE SECRETS® Onion Soup Mix***
> **4 medium all-purpose potatoes, cut into large chunks (about 2 pounds)**
> **⅓ cup olive or vegetable oil**

*Also terrific with LIPTON® RECIPE SECRETS® Onion-Mushroom, Golden Onion or Savory Herb with Garlic Soup Mix.

1. Preheat oven to 450°F. In large plastic bag or bowl, add all ingredients. Close bag and shake, or toss in bowl, until potatoes are evenly coated.

2. In 13×9-inch baking or roasting pan, arrange potatoes; discard bag.

3. Bake uncovered, stirring occasionally, 40 minutes or until potatoes are tender and golden brown.

Homestyle Spinach and Mushrooms

Makes 4 to 6 servings

> **1 packet (1 ounce) HIDDEN VALLEY® The Original Ranch® Salad Dressing & Seasoning Mix**
> **1 cup milk**
> **1 cup mayonnaise**
> **2 boxes (10 ounces *each*) frozen chopped spinach, cooked and well-drained**
> **1 jar (4.5 ounces) sliced mushrooms, drained**
> **½ cup shredded Parmesan cheese**
> **1 cup crushed croutons, for topping**

In bowl, combine dressing mix with milk and mayonnaise. Mix well. Cover and refrigerate. Chill 30 minutes to thicken. Combine dressing with remaining ingredients, except croutons, in 9-inch baking dish. Top with croutons. Bake at 325°F for 25 minutes or until thoroughly heated.

Sides of All Kinds

Onion-Roasted Potatoes

Vegetable Macaroni & Cheese

Makes about 4 servings

Cook Time: 15 to 20 minutes

> 1 box (14 ounces) macaroni and cheese
> 1 bag (16 ounces) BIRDS EYE® frozen Farm Fresh Mixtures Broccoli, Cauliflower and Carrots*

*Or, substitute any other Birds Eye® frozen Farm Fresh Mixtures variety.

Cook macaroni and cheese according to package directions. Add vegetables during last 5 minutes of cooking time. Continue preparing recipe according to package directions.

Savory Scalloped Potatoes

Makes 6 servings

> 1½ pounds all-purpose potatoes, peeled and thinly sliced
> 1 envelope LIPTON® RECIPE SECRETS® Garlic Mushroom or Savory Herb with Garlic Soup Mix
> 1 cup (8 ounces) whipping or heavy cream*
> ½ cup water

*Or, use 1 can (12 ounces) evaporated milk and eliminate water.

Preheat oven to 350°F. In lightly greased 2-quart shallow baking dish, arrange potatoes.

In medium bowl, combine remaining ingredients; pour over potatoes.

Bake, uncovered, 45 minutes or until potatoes are tender. Garnish, if desired, with chopped fresh parsley.

Sides of All Kinds

Vegetable Macaroni & Cheese

Chicken Sausage Pilaf

Makes 4 servings

1 tablespoon vegetable oil
1 pound chicken or turkey sausage, casing removed
1 cup uncooked rice and pasta mix
4 cups chicken broth
2 ribs celery, diced
¼ cup slivered almonds
Salt and black pepper to taste

Slow Cooker Directions

1. Heat oil in large skillet; add sausage. Break up sausage with back of spoon while cooking; cook until browned, about 5 minutes.

2. Add rice and pasta mix to skillet. Cook 1 minute. Place mixture in slow cooker.

3. Add remaining ingredients to slow cooker; stir well. Cover and cook on LOW 7 to 10 hours or on HIGH 3 to 4 hours or until rice is tender.

Chicken Sausage Pilaf

Ham and Cheese Corn Muffins

Makes 9 muffins

Prep and Cook Time: 30 minutes

- **1 package (about 8 ounces) corn muffin mix**
- **½ cup chopped deli ham**
- **½ cup (2 ounces) shredded Swiss cheese**
- **⅓ cup reduced-fat (2%) milk**
- **1 egg**
- **1 tablespoon Dijon mustard**

1. Preheat oven to 400°F. Combine muffin mix, ham and cheese in medium bowl.

2. Combine milk, egg and mustard in 1-cup glass measure. Stir milk mixture into dry ingredients; mix just until moistened.

3. Fill 9 paper cup-lined 2¾-inch muffin cups two-thirds full with batter.

4. Bake 18 to 20 minutes or until light golden brown. Remove muffin pan to cooling rack. Let stand 5 minutes. Serve warm.

Helpful Hint

For even more delicious flavor, serve these Ham and Cheese Corn Muffins with honey-flavored butter. Stir together equal amounts of honey and softened butter, and spread generously onto muffin halves.

Sides of All Kinds

Ham and Cheese Corn Muffins

Couscous with Vegetables in Savory Broth

Makes about 5 side-dish or 2 main-dish servings

    2 tablespoons I CAN'T BELIEVE IT'S NOT BUTTER!® Spread
    1 large onion, sliced
    ½ cup dry white wine or water
    1 cup sliced carrots
    1 medium zucchini, sliced
    1 small red or green bell pepper, sliced
    1 envelope LIPTON® RECIPE SECRETS® Savory Herb with Garlic Soup Mix
    2 cups water
  1⅓ cups (8 ounces) couscous, cooked*

*Variation: Use hot cooked penne or ziti pasta.

In 12-inch skillet, melt I Can't Believe It's Not Butter!® Spread over medium heat and cook onion, stirring occasionally, 5 minutes or until golden. Add wine and boil over high heat 1 minute. Stir in carrots, zucchini, red pepper and soup mix blended with water. Bring to a boil over high heat. Reduce heat to low and simmer uncovered, stirring occasionally, 15 minutes. To serve, spoon over hot couscous.

Menu Suggestion: Serve with a mixed green salad and sliced fresh fruit drizzled with honey for dessert.

168

Broiled Ranch Mushrooms

Makes 4 to 6 servings

    1 pound medium mushrooms
    1 packet (1 ounce) HIDDEN VALLEY® The Original Ranch® Salad Dressing
        & Seasoning Mix
    ¼ cup vegetable oil
    ¼ cup water
    1 tablespoon balsamic vinegar

Place mushrooms in a gallon-size Glad® Zipper Storage Bag. Whisk together salad dressing & seasoning mix, oil, water and vinegar. Pour over mushrooms; seal bag and marinate in refrigerator for 30 minutes, turning occasionally. Place mushrooms on a broiling rack. Broil 4 inches from heat for about 8 minutes or until tender.

Couscous with Vegetables in Savory Broth

Apple-Rice Medley

Makes 4 servings

1 package (6 ounces) long-grain and wild rice mix
1 cup (4 ounces) shredded mild Cheddar cheese, divided
1 cup chopped Washington Golden Delicious apple
1 cup sliced mushrooms
½ cup thinly sliced celery

Prepare rice mix according to package directions. Preheat oven to 350°F. Add ½ cup cheese, apple, mushrooms and celery to rice; toss to combine. Spoon mixture into 1-quart casserole dish. Bake 15 minutes. Top with remaining ½ cup cheese; bake until cheese melts, about 10 minutes.

Microwave: Combine cooked rice, ½ cup cheese, apple, mushrooms and celery as directed; spoon mixture into 1-quart microwave-safe dish. Microwave at HIGH 3 to 4 minutes or until heated through. Top with remaining ½ cup cheese; microwave at HIGH 1 minute or until cheese melts.

Favorite recipe from **Washington Apple Commission**

Helpful Hint

This dish serves as a great side to pork chops.

Apple-Rice Medley

Moist & Luscious Cakes

Chocolate Sprinkle Angel Food Cake

Makes 12 to 16 servings

1 package DUNCAN HINES® Angel Food Cake Mix
3 tablespoons chocolate sprinkles

1. Remove top rack from oven; move remaining rack to lowest position. Preheat oven to 350°F.

2. Prepare batter following package directions. Fold in chocolate sprinkles. Pour batter into *ungreased* 10-inch tube pan. Bake and cool following package directions.

Tip: For a quick finish, simply dust cake with confectioners' sugar.

Chocolate Sprinkle Angel Food Cake

Fudge Ribbon Cake

Makes 10 to 12 servings

Prep Time: 20 minutes
Bake Time: 40 minutes

- 1 (18.25-ounce) package chocolate cake mix
- 1 (8-ounce) package cream cheese, softened
- 2 tablespoons butter or margarine, softened
- 1 tablespoon cornstarch
- 1 (14-ounce) can EAGLE® BRAND Sweetened Condensed Milk (NOT evaporated milk)
- 1 egg
- 1 teaspoon vanilla extract
- Chocolate Glaze (recipe follows)

1. Preheat oven to 350°F. Grease and flour 13×9-inch baking pan. Prepare cake mix as package directs. Pour batter into prepared pan.

2. In small mixing bowl, beat cream cheese, butter and cornstarch until fluffy. Gradually beat in Eagle Brand. Add egg and vanilla; beat until smooth. Spoon evenly over cake batter.

3. Bake 40 minutes or until wooden pick inserted near center comes out clean. Cool. Prepare Chocolate Glaze and drizzle over cake. Store covered in refrigerator.

Chocolate Glaze: In small saucepan over low heat, melt 1 (1-ounce) square unsweetened or semi-sweet chocolate and 1 tablespoon butter or margarine with 2 tablespoons water. Remove from heat. Stir in ¾ cup powdered sugar and ½ teaspoon vanilla extract. Stir until smooth and well blended. Makes about ⅓ cup.

Fudge Ribbon Bundt Cake: Preheat oven to 350°F. Grease and flour 10-inch Bundt pan. Prepare cake mix as package directs. Pour batter into prepared pan. Prepare cream cheese layer as directed above; spoon evenly over batter. Bake 50 to 55 minutes or until wooden pick inserted near center comes out clean. Cool 10 minutes. Remove from pan. Cool. Prepare Chocolate Glaze and drizzle over cake. Store covered in refrigerator.

Moist & Luscious Cakes

Fudge Ribbon Cake

Peachy Cinnamon Coffeecake

Makes 9 servings

1 can (8¼ ounces) juice pack sliced yellow cling peaches
1 package DUNCAN HINES® Bakery-Style Cinnamon Swirl Muffin Mix
1 egg

1. Preheat oven to 400°F. Grease 8-inch square or 9-inch round pan.

2. Drain peaches, reserving juice. Add water to reserved juice to equal ¾ cup liquid. Chop peaches.

3. Combine muffin mix, egg and ¾ cup peach liquid in medium bowl; fold in peaches. Pour batter into pan. Knead swirl packet 10 seconds before opening. Squeeze contents onto top of batter and swirl with knife. Sprinkle topping over batter. Bake at 400°F for 28 to 33 minutes for 8-inch pan (or 20 to 25 minutes for 9-inch pan) or until golden. Serve warm.

Easy Lemon Cake

Makes 10 servings

Prep time: 20 minutes

1 package (2-layer size) lemon cake mix
1½ cups cold milk
2 packages (4-serving size each) JELL-O® Lemon *or* Vanilla Flavor Instant Pudding & Pie Filling
1 tub (8 ounces) COOL WHIP® Whipped Topping, thawed

PREPARE cake mix as directed on package for 2 (8-inch) round cake layers. Cool completely.

POUR milk into medium bowl. Add pudding mixes. Beat with wire whisk 2 minutes. Immediately spread over top of both cake layers.

PLACE one cake layer on top of the other. Frost top and side of cake with whipped topping. Refrigerate until ready to serve. Garnish as desired.

Moist & Luscious Cakes

Peachy Cinnamon Coffeecake

Carrot Cake with Easy Cream Cheese Frosting
Makes 10 servings

Prep time: 20 minutes

> 1 package (2-layer size) carrot cake mix
> 1 package (8 ounces) PHILADELPHIA® Cream Cheese, softened
> ⅓ cup granulated *or* powdered sugar
> ¼ cup cold milk
> 1 tub (8 ounces) COOL WHIP® Whipped Topping, thawed

PREPARE cake mix as directed on package for 13×9-inch pan. Cool completely.

BEAT cream cheese, sugar and milk in medium bowl with wire whisk until smooth. Gently stir in whipped topping. Spread over top of cake.

REFRIGERATE until ready to serve. Garnish as desired.

Note: Substitute your favorite carrot cake recipe for carrot cake mix.

Orange Soak Cake
Makes 12 to 16 servings

Cake
> 1 package DUNCAN HINES® Moist Deluxe® Orange Supreme Cake Mix

Glaze
> 2 cups confectioners' sugar
> ⅓ cup orange juice
> 2 tablespoons melted butter or margarine
> 1 tablespoon water

1. Preheat oven to 350°F. Grease and flour 13×9×2-inch pan.

2. For cake, prepare and bake, following package directions, for basic recipe. Poke holes in top of warm cake with tines of fork or toothpick.

3. For glaze, combine confectioners' sugar, orange juice, melted butter and water in medium bowl. Pour slowly over top, allowing glaze to soak into warm cake. Cool completely.

Tip: Sift confectioners' sugar before preparing glaze.

Moist & Luscious Cakes

Carrot Cake with Easy Cream Cheese Frosting

Easy Chocolate Pudding Cake

Makes about 16 servings

1 package (6-serving size) chocolate cook-and-serve pudding mix
3 cups milk
1 package (about 18 ounces) chocolate fudge cake mix and ingredients to prepare
Whipped topping or ice cream (optional)

Slow Cooker Directions

1. Spray inside of 4-quart slow cooker with nonstick cooking spray. Place pudding mix in slow cooker. Whisk in milk.

2. Prepare cake mix according to package directions. Carefully pour cake mix into slow cooker. Do not stir. Cover and cook on HIGH 2½ hours or until cake is set.

3. Serve warm with whipped topping or ice cream, if desired.

Coconut Cupcakes

Makes 36 cupcakes

1 package DUNCAN HINES® Moist Deluxe® Butter Recipe Golden Cake Mix
3 eggs
1 cup (8 ounces) dairy sour cream
⅔ cup cream of coconut
¼ cup butter or margarine, softened
2 containers (16 ounces each) DUNCAN HINES® Coconut Frosting

1. Preheat oven to 375°F. Place 36 (2½-inch) paper liners in muffin cups.

2. Combine cake mix, eggs, sour cream, cream of coconut and butter in large bowl. Beat at low speed until blended. Beat at medium speed 4 minutes. Fill paper liners half full. Bake 17 to 19 minutes or until toothpick inserted into center comes out clean. Cool in pans 5 minutes. Remove to cooling racks. Cool completely.

3. Frost cupcakes.

Spice Cake with Rum Caramel Sauce

Makes 12 to 16 servings

   1 package DUNCAN HINES® Moist Deluxe® Spice Cake Mix
  ¾ cup prepared caramel topping
   1 tablespoon rum or water
   1 teaspoon ground cinnamon
  ½ cup milk chocolate English toffee chips
    Whipped cream for garnish

Preheat oven to 350°F. Grease and flour 13×9-inch pan.

Prepare and bake cake as directed on package. Cool cake 10 minutes. Combine topping, rum and cinnamon in small bowl. Spread over warm cake. Top with chips. Serve warm with whipped cream, if desired.

Chocolate Cherry Angel Delight

Makes 14 servings

  ⅓ cup HERSHEY'S Cocoa
   1 package (16 ounces) angel food cake mix
   1 envelope (1.3 ounces) dry whipped topping mix
  ½ cup cold nonfat milk
  ½ teaspoon vanilla extract
   1 can (20 ounces) reduced-calorie cherry pie filling, chilled

1. Move oven rack to lowest position.

2. Sift cocoa over contents of cake mix in large bowl; stir to blend. Proceed as directed on cake mix package. Bake and cool as directed for 10-inch tube pan.

3. Carefully run knife along side of pan to loosen cake; remove from pan. Slice cake horizontally into three layers, using serrated knife.

4. Place topping mix in small, deep bowl with narrow bottom. Add ½ cup nonfat milk and ½ teaspoon vanilla; beat on high speed of mixer until stiff peaks form. Fold half the pie filling into whipped topping.

5. Place bottom cake layer on serving plate; spread with half the whipped topping mixture. Repeat layers, ending with plain cake layer on top. Spoon remaining pie filling over top. Serve immediately. Cover; refrigerate leftover cake.

Maple Praline Cheesecake

Makes 8 servings

Prep Time: 15 minutes plus refrigerating

> 1 package (11.1 ounces) JELL-O® Brand No Bake Real Cheesecake
> 2 tablespoons sugar
> 6 tablespoons butter or margarine, melted
> 1 tablespoon water
> 1⅓ cups cold milk
> ½ cup maple syrup
> 1 cup PLANTERS® Pecan Halves or Pieces
> 1 cup firmly packed brown sugar
> 1 egg, beaten

HEAT oven to 350°F.

STIR Crust Mix, sugar, butter and water thoroughly in 8- or 9-inch square baking pan until crumbs are well moistened. Firmly press crumbs onto bottom of pan, using small measuring cup.

POUR milk into large bowl. Add Filling Mix and syrup. Beat with electric mixer on lowest speed until blended. Beat on medium speed 3 minutes. (Filling will be thick.) Spoon over crust.

REFRIGERATE at least 1 hour or until set.

MIX pecans, brown sugar and beaten egg, stirring until well combined. Pour into greased 13×9-inch baking pan. Bake 10 to 12 minutes or until browned and crunchy; cool. Using spatula, loosen nut mixture from pan and chop into small pieces. Just before serving, sprinkle over cheesecake. Cut cheesecake into squares.

Serving Suggestion: To make cheesecake easier to serve, line 8- or 9-inch square pan with foil extending over edges to form handles. To serve, run knife around edges of pan to loosen cheesecake from sides. Lift cheesecake, using foil as handles, onto cutting board.

Moist & Luscious Cakes

Maple Praline Cheesecake

Cinnamon Ripple Cake

Makes 12 to 16 servings

1 package DUNCAN HINES® Angel Food Cake Mix
2¼ teaspoons ground cinnamon, divided
1½ cups frozen whipped topping, thawed

1. Preheat oven to 350°F.

2. Prepare cake following package directions. **Spoon** one-third of batter into ungreased 10-inch tube pan. **Spread** evenly. **Sprinkle** 1 teaspoon cinnamon over batter with small fine sieve. **Repeat. Top** with remaining cake batter. **Bake** and cool, following package directions.

3. Combine whipped topping and ¼ teaspoon cinnamon in small bowl. **Serve** with cake slices.

Tip: To slice cake, use a serrated knife and cut in a sawing motion.

German Chocolate Muffins

Makes 12 jumbo muffins

German Chocolate Topping (recipe follows)
1 package (18.25 ounces) pudding-included German chocolate cake mix

Preheat oven to 400°F. Grease 12 (3½-inch) large muffin cups; set aside. Prepare German Chocolate Topping; set aside.

Prepare cake mix according to package directions, *reducing* water by ¼ cup. Spoon into prepared muffin cups, filling half full. Sprinkle German Chocolate Topping evenly over tops of muffins.

Bake 20 to 25 minutes or until toothpick inserted into center comes out clean. Cool in pan on wire rack 5 minutes. Remove from pan. Cool on wire rack 10 minutes. Serve warm or cool completely.

German Chocolate Topping: Combine 3 tablespoons *each* chopped pecans, flaked coconut and packed brown sugar in small bowl until well blended.

Moist & Luscious Cakes

Cinnamon Ripple Cake

Fudgey Chocolate Cupcakes

Makes 16 cupcakes

¾ cup water
½ cup (1 stick) 60% vegetable oil spread, melted
2 egg whites, slightly beaten
1 teaspoon vanilla extract
2¼ cups HERSHEY₅S Basic Cocoa Baking Mix (recipe follows)
2 teaspoons powdered sugar
2 teaspoons HERSHEY₅S Cocoa (optional)

1. Heat oven to 350°F. Line 16 muffin cups (2½ inches in diameter) with foil or paper baking cups.

2. Stir together water, melted spread, egg whites and vanilla in large bowl. Add Basic Cocoa Baking Mix; beat on low speed of mixer until blended. Fill muffin cups ⅔ full with batter.

3. Bake 20 to 25 minutes or until wooden pick inserted into centers comes out clean. Remove from pans to wire racks. Cool completely. Sift powdered sugar over tops of cupcakes. If desired, partially cover part of each cupcake with paper cutout. Sift cocoa over exposed powdered sugar. Carefully lift off cutout. Store, covered, at room temperature.

Hershey₅s Basic Cocoa Baking Mix: Stir together 4½ cups all-purpose flour, 2¾ cups sugar, 1¼ cups HERSHEY₅S Cocoa, 1 tablespoon plus ½ teaspoon baking powder, 1¾ teaspoons salt and 1¼ teaspoons baking soda. Store in airtight container in cool, dry place for up to 1 month. Stir before using. Makes 8 cups mix.

Moist & Luscious Cakes

Fudgey Chocolate Cupcakes

Spring Break Blueberry Coffeecake

Makes 9 servings

Topping
  ½ cup flaked coconut
  ¼ cup firmly packed brown sugar
  2 tablespoons butter or margarine, softened
  1 tablespoon all-purpose flour
Cake
  1 package DUNCAN HINES® Bakery-Style Wild Maine Blueberry Muffin Mix
  1 can (8 ounces) crushed pineapple with juice, undrained
  1 egg
  ¼ cup water

1. Preheat oven to 350°F. Grease 9-inch square pan.

2. For Topping, combine coconut, brown sugar, butter and flour in small bowl. Mix with fork until well blended. Set aside.

3. Rinse blueberries from Mix with cold water and drain.

4. For Cake, place muffin mix in medium bowl. Break up any lumps. Add pineapple with juice, egg and water. Stir until moistened, about 50 strokes. Fold in blueberries. Spread in pan. Sprinkle reserved topping over batter. Bake at 350°F for 30 to 35 minutes or until toothpick inserted into center comes out clean. Serve warm, or cool completely.

Helpful Hint

To keep blueberries from discoloring the batter, drain them on paper towels after rinsing.

Moist & Luscious Cakes

Spring Break Blueberry Coffeecake

More Sweets, Please!

Layer After Layer Lemon Pie
Makes 8 servings

Prep Time: 20 minutes plus refrigerating

⅓ cup strawberry jam
1 HONEY MAID® Honey Graham Pie Crust (9 inch)
4 ounces PHILADELPHIA® Cream Cheese, softened
1 tablespoon sugar
1 tub (8 ounces) COOL WHIP® Whipped Topping, thawed, divided
1½ cups cold milk or half-and-half
2 packages (4-serving size each) JELL-O® Lemon Flavor Instant Pudding & Pie Filling
2 teaspoons grated lemon peel

SPREAD jam gently onto bottom of pie crust.

MIX cream cheese and sugar in large bowl with wire whisk until smooth. Gently stir in ½ of the whipped topping. Spread on top of jam.

POUR milk into large bowl. Add pudding mixes and lemon peel. Beat with wire whisk 1 minute. (Mixture will be thick.) Gently stir in remaining whipped topping. Spread over cream cheese layer.

REFRIGERATE 4 hours or until set. Garnish with additional whipped topping, if desired.

Magic Cookie Bars

Makes 2 to 3 dozen bars

Prep Time: 10 minutes
Bake Time: 25 minutes

½ cup (1 stick) butter or margarine
1½ cups graham cracker crumbs
1 (14-ounce) can EAGLE® BRAND Sweetened Condensed Milk
    (NOT evaporated milk)
2 cups (12 ounces) semi-sweet chocolate chips
1⅓ cups flaked coconut
1 cup chopped nuts

1. Preheat oven to 350°F (325°F for glass dish). In 13×9-inch baking pan, melt butter in oven.

2. Sprinkle crumbs over butter; pour Eagle Brand evenly over crumbs. Layer evenly with remaining ingredients; press down firmly.

3. Bake 25 minutes or until lightly browned. Cool. Chill, if desired. Cut into bars. Store loosely covered at room temperature.

7-Layer Magic Cookie Bars: Substitute 1 cup (6 ounces) butterscotch-flavored chips, peanut butter-flavored chips or white chocolate chips for 1 cup semi-sweet chocolate chips.

Magic Peanut Cookie Bars: Substitute 2 cups (about ¾ pound) chocolate-covered peanuts for semi-sweet chocolate chips and chopped nuts.

Magic Rainbow Cookie Bars: Substitute 2 cups plain candy-coated chocolate pieces for semi-sweet chocolate chips.

More Sweets, Please!

Top to bottom: Magic Cookie Bars, Magic Rainbow Cookie Bars

Strawberry Cheesecake Pudding Pie

Makes 8 servings

Prep Time: 10 minutes
Chilling Time: 3 hours

1½ cups strawberry, cherry or raspberry pie filling, divided
1 (6-ounce) READY CRUST® Graham Cracker Pie Crust
1½ cups cold milk
2 (4-serving size each) packages JELL-O® Cheesecake Flavor Instant Pudding & Pie Filling
1 (8-ounce) tub COOL WHIP® Whipped Topping, thawed

1. Spoon ½ cup fruit pie filling into crust.

2. Pour milk into large bowl. Add pudding mixes. Beat with wire whisk 2 minutes or until smooth. (Mixture will be thick.) Immediately stir in whipped topping. Spoon over pie filling in crust.

3. Refrigerate 3 hours or until set. Top with remaining pie filling. Garnish as desired. Refrigerate leftovers.

194

Helpful Hint

To thaw a frozen 8-ounce tub of COOL WHIP® Whipped Topping, store it, unopened, in the refrigerator for 4 hours.

More Sweets, Please!

Strawberry Cheesecake Pudding Pie

Blueberry Cheesecake Bars

Makes about 16 bars

> 1 package DUNCAN HINES® Bakery-Style Blueberry Streusel Muffin Mix
> ¼ cup cold butter or margarine
> ⅓ cup finely chopped pecans
> 1 (8-ounce) package cream cheese, softened
> ½ cup sugar
> 1 egg
> 3 tablespoons lemon juice
> 1 teaspoon grated lemon peel

1. Preheat oven to 350°F. Grease 9-inch square pan.

2. Rinse blueberries from Mix with cold water and drain; set aside.

3. Place muffin mix in medium bowl; cut in butter with pastry blender or two knives. Stir in pecans. Press into bottom of prepared pan. Bake 15 minutes or until set.

4. Combine cream cheese and sugar in medium bowl. Beat until smooth. Add egg, lemon juice and lemon peel. Beat well. Spread over baked crust. Sprinkle with blueberries. Sprinkle topping packet from Mix over blueberries. Return to oven. Bake 35 to 40 minutes or until filling is set. Cool completely. Refrigerate until ready to serve. Cut into bars.

Helpful Hint

Pecans can be stored in an airtight container up to 3 months in the refrigerator and up to 6 months in the freezer.

More Sweets, Please!

Blueberry Cheesecake Bars

Creamy Chocolate Pie
Makes 8 servings

Preparation Time: 10 minutes
Refrigerating Time: 4 hours

   1¾ **cups cold milk**
     2 **packages (4-serving size each) JELL-O® Chocolate or Chocolate Fudge**
         Flavor Instant Pudding & Pie Filling
     1 **tub (8 ounces) COOL WHIP® Whipped Topping, thawed**
     1 **prepared chocolate flavor crumb crust (6 ounces)**

POUR milk into large bowl. Add pudding mixes. Beat with wire whisk until well mixed. (Mixture will be thick.) Immediately stir in whipped topping. Spoon into crust.

REFRIGERATE 4 hours or until set. Garnish as desired.

Vanilla Butter Crescents
Makes 4 dozen cookies

     1 **package DUNCAN HINES® Moist Deluxe® French Vanilla Cake Mix**
   ¾ **cup butter, softened**
     1 **vanilla bean, very finely chopped (see Tip)**
     1 **cup finely chopped pecans or walnuts**
      Confectioners' sugar

1. Preheat oven to 350°F.

2. Place cake mix and butter in large bowl. Cut in butter with pastry blender or 2 knives. Stir in vanilla bean and pecans. Since mixture is crumbly, it may be helpful to work dough with hands to blend until mixture holds together. Shape dough into balls. Roll 1 ball between palms until 4 inches long. Shape into crescent. Repeat with remaining balls. Place 2 inches apart on ungreased baking sheets. Bake at 350°F for 10 to 12 minutes or until light golden brown around edges. Cool 2 minutes on baking sheets. Remove to cooling racks. Dust with confectioners' sugar. Cool completely. Dust with additional confectioners' sugar, if desired. Store in airtight container.

Tip: To quickly chop vanilla bean, place in work bowl of food processor fitted with knife blade. Process until fine.

More Sweets, Please!

Creamy Chocolate Pie

Strawberry Shortcakes

Makes 6 servings

Prep Time: 6 minutes
Bake Time: 12 minutes

½ cup sugar
1 quart sliced strawberries (about 4 cups)
2⅓ cups BISQUICK® Original Baking Mix
½ cup milk
3 tablespoons butter or margarine, melted
3 tablespoons sugar
1 tub (8 ounces) COOL WHIP® Whipped Topping, thawed

HEAT oven to 425°F.

MIX ½ cup sugar into strawberries; set aside. Stir baking mix, milk, butter and 3 tablespoons sugar in bowl until soft dough forms. Drop by 6 spoonfuls onto ungreased cookie sheet.

BAKE 10 to 12 minutes or until golden brown. Split warm shortcakes; fill and top with strawberries and whipped topping.

Tip: For a more decadent dessert, try adding 1 cup BAKER'S® Semi-Sweet Chocolate Chunks into the baking mix and proceed as directed above. Drizzle with your favorite chocolate sauce.

More Sweets, Please!

Strawberry Shortcake

Chocolate Chip Waffles

Makes 10 to 12 waffles

> 1 package DUNCAN HINES® Chocolate Chip Muffin Mix
> ¾ cup all-purpose flour
> 1 teaspoon baking powder
> 1¾ cups milk
> 2 eggs
> 5 tablespoons butter or margarine, melted
> Confectioners' sugar (optional)

Preheat and lightly grease waffle iron according to manufacturer's directions.

Combine muffin mix, flour and baking powder in large bowl. Add milk, eggs and melted butter. Stir until moistened, about 50 strokes. Pour batter onto center grids of preheated waffle iron. Bake according to manufacturer's directions until golden brown. Remove baked waffle carefully with fork. Repeat with remaining batter. Dust lightly with confectioners' sugar, if desired. Top with fresh fruit, syrup, grated chocolate or whipped cream, if desired.

"BaNilla" Cookie Pie

Makes 8 servings

Prep Time: 10 minutes plus refrigerating

> 2½ cups cold milk
> 2 packages (4-serving size each) JELL-O® Banana *or* Vanilla Flavor Instant Pudding & Pie Filling
> 1 large ripe banana, diced
> 1 cup chopped NUTTER BUTTER® Cookies
> 1 tub (8 ounces) COOL WHIP® Whipped Topping, thawed, divided
> 1 NILLA® Pie Crust (9 inch)
> NUTTER BUTTER® Cookie halves for garnish (optional)

POUR milk into large bowl. Add pudding mixes. Beat with wire whisk 2 minutes or until well blended. (Mixture will be thick.) Gently stir in banana pieces, chopped cookies and ½ of the whipped topping. Spoon into crust.

REFRIGERATE 3 hours or until set. Garnish with remaining whipped topping and cookie halves.

Hint: Try chopped and halved NILLA® Wafers or LORNA DOONE® Shortbread instead of NUTTER BUTTER® Cookies.

More Sweets, Please!

Chocolate Chip Waffles

Butterscotch Pan Cookies

Makes 48 bars

> 1 package DUNCAN HINES® Moist Deluxe® French Vanilla Cake Mix
> 2 eggs
> 1 cup butter or margarine, melted
> ¾ cup firmly packed light brown sugar
> 1 teaspoon vanilla extract
> 1 package (12 ounces) butterscotch flavored chips
> 1½ cups chopped pecans

1. Preheat oven to 375°F. Grease 15½×10½×1-inch jelly-roll pan.

2. Combine cake mix, eggs, melted butter, brown sugar and vanilla extract in large bowl. Beat at low speed with electric mixer until smooth and creamy. Stir in butterscotch chips and pecans. Spread in pan. Bake at 375°F for 20 to 25 minutes or until golden brown. Cool completely. Cut into bars.

Tip: You can substitute chocolate or peanut butter flavored chips for the butterscotch flavored chips.

Quick Chocolate Mousse

Makes 8 to 10 servings

Prep Time: 5 minutes

> 1 (14-ounce) can EAGLE® BRAND Sweetened Condensed Milk
>   (NOT evaporated milk)
> 1 (4-serving-size) package instant chocolate pudding and pie filling mix
> 1 cup cold water
> 1 cup (½ pint) whipping cream, whipped

1. In large mixing bowl, beat Eagle Brand, pudding mix and water; chill 5 minutes.

2. Fold in whipped cream. Spoon into serving dishes; chill. Garnish as desired.

More Sweets, Please!

Quick Chocolate Chip Cookie Cakes

Makes 4 dozen cookies

- 1 package (18.25 ounces) reduced-fat yellow cake mix
- ½ cup cholesterol-free egg substitute
- ¼ cup vegetable oil
- ¼ cup reduced-fat sour cream
- 2 cups uncooked old-fashioned oats
- ½ cup reduced-fat semisweet chocolate chips

1. Preheat oven to 350°F. Lightly coat cookie sheet with nonstick cooking spray; set aside.

2. Combine cake mix, egg substitute, oil and sour cream in medium bowl. Add oats and chocolate chips.

3. Drop dough by even teaspoonfuls onto prepared cookie sheet.

4. Bake 12 minutes or until lightly browned. Remove to wire rack and cool completely.

Decadent Chocolate Cream Pie

Makes 8 servings

Prep Time: 10 minutes plus refrigerating

- 2 packages (4-serving size each) JELL-O® Chocolate Flavor Cook & Serve Pudding & Pie Filling (not Instant)
- 3½ cups half-and-half
- 1 baked pastry shell (9 inch), cooled
- 1 tub (8 ounces) COOL WHIP® Whipped Topping, thawed

STIR pudding mixes and half-and-half in medium saucepan with wire whisk until blended. Stirring constantly, cook over medium heat until mixture comes to full boil. Pour into pastry shell.

REFRIGERATE 3 hours or until set. Garnish pie with whipped topping.

Tip: Use an OREO® Pie Crust (9 inch) instead of a pastry shell. Garnish pie with chocolate shavings or chocolate sprinkles.

More Sweets, Please!

Juicy Triple Berry Pie

Makes 8 servings

Preparation Time: 20 minutes
Refrigerating Time: 3 hours

> 3 cups assorted berries
> 1 graham cracker crumb or shortbread pie crust (6 ounces)
> ½ cup sugar
> 2 tablespoons cornstarch
> 1½ cups orange or orange strawberry banana juice
> 1 package (4-serving size) JELL-O® Brand Gelatin, any red flavor

ARRANGE berries in crust.

MIX sugar and cornstarch in medium saucepan. Gradually stir in juice until smooth. Stirring constantly, cook on medium heat until mixture comes to a boil; boil 1 minute. Remove from heat. Stir in gelatin until completely dissolved. Cool to room temperature; pour into crust.

REFRIGERATE 3 hours or until firm. Garnish with COOL WHIP®, if desired. Store leftover pie in refrigerator.

Helpful Hint

Try using a combination of blueberries, raspberries and strawberries in this recipe. Or, use only one type of berry and serve up a delicious single-berry Triple-Berry Pie!

More Sweets, Please!

Juicy Triple Berry Pie

Cindy's Fudgy Brownies

Makes 24 brownies

   1 (21-ounce) package DUNCAN HINES® Family-Style Chewy Fudge
      Brownie Mix
   1 egg
   ⅓ cup water
   ⅓ cup vegetable oil
   ¾ cup semi-sweet chocolate chips
   ½ cup chopped pecans

1. Preheat oven to 350°F. Grease bottom of 13×9×2-inch pan.

2. Combine brownie mix, egg, water and oil in large bowl. Stir with spoon until well blended, about 50 strokes. Stir in chocolate chips. Spread in pan. Sprinkle with pecans. Bake at 350°F 25 to 28 minutes or until set. Cool completely. Cut into bars.

Helpful Hint

Overbaking brownies will cause them to become dry. Closely follow the recommended baking times given in recipes.

208

More Sweets, Please!

SAURUS

TRICERATOPS

Cindy's Fudgy Brownies

Creamy Banana Pudding

Makes 8 to 10 servings

Prep Time: 15 minutes

    1 (14-ounce) can EAGLE® BRAND Sweetened Condensed Milk
        (NOT evaporated milk)
  1½ cups cold water
    1 (4-serving size) package instant vanilla pudding and pie filling mix
    2 cups (1 pint) whipping cream, whipped
  36 vanilla wafers
    3 medium bananas, sliced and dipped in lemon juice from concentrate

1. In large mixing bowl, combine Eagle Brand and water. Add pudding mix; beat until well blended. Chill 5 minutes.

2. Fold in whipped cream. Spoon 1 cup pudding mixture into 2½-quart glass serving bowl.

3. Top with one-third each of vanilla wafers, bananas and pudding mixture. Repeat layering twice, ending with pudding mixture. Chill thoroughly. Garnish as desired. Refrigerate leftovers.

Helpful Hint

For best results when beating whipping cream, chill the cream, bowl and beaters first. The cold temperature keeps the fat in the cream solid, thus increasing the whipped cream's volume.

Creamy Banana Pudding

Rice Delight Dessert

Makes 8 servings

1 bag SUCCESS® Rice
1 can (15 ounces) peach halves in juice, undrained
1 can (5½ ounces) pineapple tidbits in juice, undrained
   Skim milk (about 1¼ cups)
1 package (5.1 ounces) vanilla instant pudding and pie filling mix
2 cups miniature marshmallows
1 cup chopped nuts (optional)
2 cups seedless grapes, halved
⅓ cup maraschino cherries, halved

Prepare rice according to package directions. Cool.

Drain peaches and pineapple, reserving juices; chop peaches. Combine peach and pineapple juices in 2-cup measuring cup. Add enough skim milk to juices to measure 2 cups. Combine pudding mix and juice mixture in medium bowl; beat until well blended. Stir in rice and remaining ingredients. Chill. Serve in hollowed out pineapple shell, if desired.

Peachy Blueberry Crunch

Makes 9 servings

1 package DUNCAN HINES® Bakery-Style Blueberry Streusel Muffin Mix
4 cups sliced peeled peaches (about 4 large)
½ cup water
3 tablespoons packed brown sugar
½ cup chopped pecans
⅓ cup butter or margarine, melted
   Whipped topping or ice cream (optional)

Preheat oven to 350°F.

Rinse blueberries from Mix with cold water and drain.

Arrange peach slices into *ungreased* 9-inch square pan. Sprinkle blueberries over peaches. Combine water and sugar in small bowl. Pour over fruit.

Combine muffin mix, pecans and melted butter in large bowl. Stir until thoroughly blended (mixture will be crumbly). Sprinkle crumb mixture over fruit. Sprinkle contents of topping packet from mix over crumb mixture. Bake 50 to 55 minutes or until lightly browned and bubbly. Serve warm with whipped topping, if desired.

More Sweets, Please!

Rice Delight Dessert

Easy Lemon Cookies

Makes 4 dozen cookies

> 1 package DUNCAN HINES® Moist Deluxe® Lemon Cake Mix
> 2 eggs
> ½ cup vegetable oil
> 1 teaspoon grated lemon peel
> Pecan halves, for garnish

1. Preheat oven to 350°F.

2. Combine cake mix, eggs, oil and lemon peel in large bowl. Stir until thoroughly blended. Drop by rounded teaspoonfuls 2 inches apart onto ungreased cookie sheets. Press pecan half in center of each cookie. Bake 9 to 11 minutes or until edges are light golden brown. Cool 1 minute on cookie sheets. Remove to wire racks. Cool completely. Store in airtight container.

Tip: You may substitute whole almonds or walnut halves for the pecan halves.

5-Minute Double Layer Pie

Makes 8 servings

Preparation Time: 5 minutes

> 1¼ cups cold milk
> 2 packages (4-serving size each) JELL-O® Instant Pudding, Chocolate Flavor, Lemon Flavor or other flavor
> 1 tub (8 ounces) COOL WHIP® Whipped Topping, thawed, divided
> 1 prepared graham cracker crumb crust or chocolate pie crust (6 ounces or 9 inches)

BEAT milk, pudding mixes and ½ of whipped topping in medium bowl with wire whisk 1 minute (mixture will be thick). Spread in crust.

SPREAD remaining whipped topping over pudding layer in crust. Refrigerate until ready to serve.

More Sweets, Please!

Easy Lemon Cookies

Quick and Easy Jumbles

Makes about 2 dozen cookies

> 1 package (about 17 ounces) sugar cookie mix
> ½ cup butter, melted
> 1 egg, lightly beaten
> ½ cup mini candy coated chocolate pieces *or* ½ cup semisweet chocolate chips
> ½ cup raisins
> ½ cup coarsely chopped walnuts

1. Preheat oven to 350°F.

2. Combine cookie mix, butter and egg in large bowl. Stir with spoon until well blended. Stir in chocolate pieces, raisins and walnuts.

3. Drop dough by rounded teaspoonfuls onto *ungreased* cookie sheets about 2 inches apart. Bake for 7 to 8 minutes or until set. Cool 1 minute on sheets. Remove cookies to wire racks; cool completely.

More Sweets, Please!

Creamy Banana Toffee Dessert

Makes 12 to 14 servings

1 package DUNCAN HINES® Moist Deluxe Butter Recipe Golden Cake Mix
1 (4-serving-size) package banana cream-flavor instant pudding and pie
    filling mix
1½ cups milk
1 (8-ounce) container frozen non-dairy whipped topping, thawed
3 medium bananas, sliced
¾ cup English toffee bits

Preheat oven to 375°F. Grease and flour 10-inch tube pan.

Prepare, bake and cool cake as directed on package. Meanwhile, combine pudding mix and milk in medium bowl. Chill 5 minutes. Fold in whipped topping. Chill while cake cools.

To assemble, cut cake into 12 slices. Place 6 cake slices in 3-quart clear glass bowl. Top with half of bananas, puding and toffee bits. Repeat layering. Chill until ready to serve.

Helpful Hint

Keep sliced bananas from turning brown by dipping them in lemon juice before adding them to the dish.

More Sweets, Please!

Acknowledgments

The publisher would like to thank the companies and organizations listed below for the use of their recipes and photographs in this publication.

Birds Eye®

Bob Evans®

Del Monte Corporation

Duncan Hines® and Moist Deluxe® are registered trademarks of Aurora Foods Inc.

Eagle® Brand

The Fremont Company, Makers of Frank's & SnowFloss Kraut and Tomato Products

The Golden Grain Company®

Hershey Foods Corporation

The Hidden Valley® Food Products Company

Hillshire Farm®

Keebler® Company

Kraft Foods Holdings

Lawry's® Foods, Inc.

McIlhenny Company (TABASCO® brand Pepper Sauce)

National Turkey Federation

Nestlé USA

Reckitt Benckiser Inc.

Riviana Foods Inc.

StarKist® Seafood Company

Tyson Foods, Inc.

Uncle Ben's Inc.

Unilever Bestfoods North America

Veg•All®

Washington Apple Commission

Index

220

Index

E

Easy "Baked" Beans, 164
Easy Beef Stroganoff, 90
Easy Chocolate Pudding Cake, 180
Easy Ham & Veg•All® Chowder, 60
Easy Lemon Cake, 176
Easy Lemon Cookies, 214
Easy Pasta Bake with Vegetables, 138
Extra Special Spinach Dip, 26

F

Fast 'n Easy Chili, 56
Fiesta Salad, 78
5-Minute Beef & Asparagus Stir-Fry, 100
5-Minute Double Layer Pie, 214
Foolproof Clam Fettuccine, 135
French-Style Pizza Bites (Pissaladière), 8
Fresco Marinated Chicken, 118
Fresh Vegetable Sauté, 150
Fudge Ribbon Bundt Cake, 174
Fudge Ribbon Cake, 174
Fudgey Chocolate Cupcakes, 186

G

Garden Garlic Burgers, 114
Garlic Black Beans & Rice, 152
Garlic Chicken, 110
Garlic Mashed Potatoes, 154
Garlic Toasts, 38
German Chocolate Muffins, 184
German Chocolate Topping, 184
Grilled Swordfish Steaks, 114
Grilled Vegetable Platter, 108

H

Ham and Cheese Corn Muffins, 166
Harvest Pot Roast with Sweet Potatoes, 142
Hash Brown Bake, 148
Hearty Lentil Stew, 53
Hearty Minestrone Soup, 42
Hearty Mushroom Barley Soup, 58
Hearty One-Pot Chicken Stew, 58
Hearty White Bean Soup, 62
Herbed Blue Cheese Spread with Garlic Toasts, 38
Hershey's Basic Cocoa Baking Mix, 186
Hidden Valley® Bacon-Cheddar Ranch Dip, 30
Hidden Valley® Glazed Baby Carrots, 152
Hidden Valley® Salsa Ranch Dip, 22
Homestyle Spinach and Mushrooms, 160
Honey-Lime Pork Chops, 106
Hot 'n' Spicy Italian Stix Mix, 26
Hot Artichoke Dip, 12
Hot French Onion Dip, 32

I

Indian Summer Turkey Soup, 42
Italian Vegetables with Garlic Butter Rice, 156

J

Juicy Triple Berry Pie, 206

L

Layer After Layer Lemon Pie, 190
Lemon-Twist Chicken, 132
Lipton® Onion Burgers, 112
Lipton® Onion Dip, 36
Lipton® Ranch Dip, 36

M

Magic Cookie Bars, 192
Magic Peanut Cookie Bars, 192
Magic Rainbow Cookie Bars, 192
Mama's Best Ever Spaghetti & Meatballs, 132
Maple Praline Cheesecake, 182
Meatball & Pasta Soup, 60
Mediterranean Orzo Salad, 74
Melon Salad, 82
Mexicali Cornbread Casserole, 88
Mexicali Vegetable Soup, 52
Mexicana Marinade Paste, 112
Mission Ensenada Fish Tacos, 115
Mississippi Barbecue Burgers, 118
Mushroom-Beef Stew, 44
Mushrooms
  Apple-Rice Medley, 170
  Broiled Ranch Mushrooms, 168
  Creamy Turkey Soup, 54
  Foolproof Clam Fettuccine, 135
  Grilled Vegetable Platter, 108
  Homestyle Spinach and Mushrooms, 160
  Mushroom-Beef Stew, 44
  Oriental Shrimp & Steak Kabobs, 104
  Oriental Turkey Noodle Salad, 82
  Stuffed Mushrooms, 20
  Turkey Tetrazzini, 134

N

Nuts
  Butterscotch Pan Cookies, 204
  Cheddar Cheese and Rice Roll, 18
  Cindy's Fudgy Brownies, 208
  Magic Cookie Bars, 192
  Magic Peanut Cookie Bars, 192
  Magic Rainbow Cookie Bars, 192
  Maple Praline Cheesecake, 182
  Ortega® Snack Mix, 22
  Peachy Blueberry Crunch, 212
  Peanut Chicken Stir-Fry, 84
  Quick and Easy Jumbles, 216
  7-Layer Magic Cookie Bars, 192
  Vanilla Butter Crescents, 198

O

Onion-Roasted Potatoes, 160
Oniony Corn Muffins, 154
Orange Soak Cake, 178

221

Index

Index

223

Index

METRIC CONVERSION CHART

VOLUME MEASUREMENTS (dry)

1/8 teaspoon = 0.5 mL
1/4 teaspoon = 1 mL
1/2 teaspoon = 2 mL
3/4 teaspoon = 4 mL
1 teaspoon = 5 mL
1 tablespoon = 15 mL
2 tablespoons = 30 mL
1/4 cup = 60 mL
1/3 cup = 75 mL
1/2 cup = 125 mL
2/3 cup = 150 mL
3/4 cup = 175 mL
1 cup = 250 mL
2 cups = 1 pint = 500 mL
3 cups = 750 mL
4 cups = 1 quart = 1 L

VOLUME MEASUREMENTS (fluid)

1 fluid ounce (2 tablespoons) = 30 mL
4 fluid ounces (1/2 cup) = 125 mL
8 fluid ounces (1 cup) = 250 mL
12 fluid ounces (1 1/2 cups) = 375 mL
16 fluid ounces (2 cups) = 500 mL

WEIGHTS (mass)

1/2 ounce = 15 g
1 ounce = 30 g
3 ounces = 90 g
4 ounces = 120 g
8 ounces = 225 g
10 ounces = 285 g
12 ounces = 360 g
16 ounces = 1 pound = 450 g

DIMENSIONS

1/16 inch = 2 mm
1/8 inch = 3 mm
1/4 inch = 6 mm
1/2 inch = 1.5 cm
3/4 inch = 2 cm
1 inch = 2.5 cm

OVEN TEMPERATURES

250°F = 120°C
275°F = 140°C
300°F = 150°C
325°F = 160°C
350°F = 180°C
375°F = 190°C
400°F = 200°C
425°F = 220°C
450°F = 230°C

BAKING PAN SIZES

Utensil	Size in Inches/Quarts	Metric Volume	Size in Centimeters
Baking or Cake Pan (square or rectangular)	8×8×2	2 L	20×20×5
	9×9×2	2.5 L	23×23×5
	12×8×2	3 L	30×20×5
	13×9×2	3.5 L	33×23×5
Loaf Pan	8×4×3	1.5 L	20×10×7
	9×5×3	2 L	23×13×7
Round Layer Cake Pan	8×1½	1.2 L	20×4
	9×1½	1.5 L	23×4
Pie Plate	8×1¼	750 mL	20×3
	9×1¼	1 L	23×3
Baking Dish or Casserole	1 quart	1 L	—
	1½ quart	1.5 L	—
	2 quart	2 L	—